When the housing market began to collapse in late 2007 many, including professional investors, were unprepared for exactly what that would mean in terms of personal and investment properties.

Home values quickly devalued, mortgage rates adjusted, millions were suddenly unemployed, and houses went into foreclosure at a rate not seen since the Great Depression of the 1930s.

As someone who has lived through the worst circumstances of these current trying times, Anthony Biagi realized that there was no one single place where he could get the information he needed regarding the steps that are available for someone in foreclosure, underwater on their mortgage, or both, as well as how to repair damaged credit. This is that book. Everything you need to know about the foreclosure process or dealing with an underwater property is here, compiled in one place, to help you steer your way through the challenging waters of the foreclosure and underwater mortgage financial storm.

The Homeowner Blueprint:

Navigating the Real Estate Storm

Anthony Biagi

HelpwithHouses.com

A Lucky Bat Book

The Homeowner Blueprint:
Navigating the Real Estate Storm

Cover Artist: Shawn Hand
Author Photos: Jeramie Lu Photography
Building Silhouettes graphic: Phanlop88
Splash Bubble photo: Zole4
Interior design: Theresa Rose

ISBN: 978-1-939051-43-1

Published by Lucky Bat Books
10 9 8 7 6 5 4 3 2 1

Visit the author's website at HelpwithHouses.com.

However, if you know of someone who could benefit or be helped by the information contained in this book, please, share the book or the information with them. My goal is to help as many people with real estate difficulties as possible. Thank you. —AB

Dedication

To all those homeowners who have fallen victim to the recent *Real Estate Market Crash,* this book is dedicated to you. I know how it feels to lose a home, and I hope and pray that this book will help you find salvation as you determine how to resolve your real estate related issues and prevent them from further burdening your life.

Acknowledgements

I have so many reasons to be thankful. Without the rock-star power team I have surrounding me and assisting me in every way to become successful, the helpful vision I see for homeowners would not be possible.

My mother, Laurie Biagi, supports and believes in me the way a perfect mother does, she has given me the world. Rebecka Hinson shares the most important thing in the world with me, our beautiful daughter, Arabella Biagi, and supports me unconditionally. I hope I make her feel the same way. She and my mom share the award for the best moms I know. Ryan Evanson and Lena and Shawn Van Asdale are true friends that always lead me in the right direction. Auntie Beth and Lydia, knowing that I have your support and encouragement, in good times and bad, has made all the difference. Lastly, my Uncle Dan has always believed in me and continues to give me the passion and confidence to be completely me. When I need fatherly advice, and the man upstairs is not passing me notes from my dad, Uncle Dan is my man.

From the beginning of Help with Houses, my friend David Blaco saw my vision and helped me to get my thoughts in clear form. My first employee and now business partner and advisor, Anne Cates, organizes me and my business and assists in many ways with her experience in personal retirement counseling, account collections and business formation. She is invaluable and a Reno/Sparks insider having grown up and raised her family here. My first personal coach and mentor, Jonathan Lynas, steps up in every way when my team needs something. He helps make my dreams become reality and he keeps me moving forward. Many other team members at Help with Houses contribute the little things that make so many big changes possible for homeowners. I thank them all for their past and future contributions. Homeowners need so much help and it takes a team to dream this big.

Julie Ricks and Cindie Geddes, your work is exceptional and it has made the editing and publishing process easy for a newcomer in the industry. Garrett Sutton, your guidance is truly invaluable, and Raymond Aaron, I greatly appreciate the system you have taught me.

I would also like to thank the very generous people who allowed me to use photos of their homes or private properties in the book.

Finally, I want to thank Pastor Goudeaux, for channeling the man up above and empowering me to write this book. I hope and pray it helps save others from the hardships I have endured. Without a direction, I lost homes and made some decisions I would take back and correct if I could. The most that I can do is tell my story and hope it helps others in need. When you are ready for help, the door at Help with Houses will be open.

Thank you in advance for reading this book and sharing it with someone who may need it more than you do. This information can benefit anyone who reads it; so please pass it along to friends you care about. Thank you again. Thank you, everyone.

—Anthony Biagi

Contents

Introduction

There is an ancient Chinese curse, which although neither Chinese nor ancient, has the ring of universal truth in its modest words:

May you live in interesting times.

I am sure every generation can make the claim that its lifetime was the most interesting and dramatic. Certainly, historians will pick over the wreckage of the last seven years as a benchmark of rapid transformative changes in social structure, economics, and culture that has not been seen at any other time in human history—likely since the industrial revolution.

The reasons for these changes are varied and inconstant, but the result has been the same: Global destabilization of economies and finances.

The United States was just as affected as most other first–world nations. Many good hardworking Americans became drawn into the disaster that was the sub–prime mortgage bubble and collapse through no fault of their own. Many of these upright individuals navigated the labyrinthine path to home ownership, a path they quite often barely understood, but simply nodded their heads in acquiescence and kept signing documents until someone handed them the keys to their house.

Purchasing a home in normal circumstances can be a confusing, lengthy, and emotional process full of legalese and bulky paperwork that the average person untrained in real estate or the mortgage industry does not understand. New homebuyers put their trust in their banker's hands and hoped for the best. The bankers were "the experts" the buyers felt, the people they could turn to for help and answers.

These same homebuyers soon found themselves struggling financially, possibly in foreclosure, with their homes underwater, or both, but where were they to turn for help to negotiate the treacherous waters of this mysterious, scary, and perplexing process?

There are plenty of people that are happy to assist you during your home buying process, but who will help you when you get in trouble with that house? You may search only to discover that you are on your own.

Anthony Biagi found himself in this same predicament when his tenants were unable to continue making rental payments—payments he used to pay the mortgages on his properties. He found no one with the answers he needed to get through the housing bubble collapse as simply and as quickly as possible. He had to discover solutions on his own.

As an attorney and Rich Dad Advisor, I talk to people struggling with their mortgages every day. I can tell them that Anthony has been in their shoes, and this is why I am excited to introduce his book to you. He has knowledgeable, clear, no–nonsense information, written in layman's terms without a bunch of jargon or legal terms that the average in–trouble homeowner may not be familiar understand. He is the guy with the answers.

He carefully lays out all the options available to you if you are:

- In foreclosure
- Underwater, i.e., owe more on your home than its current value
- Both

He also offers solid advice on how to rebuild your credit and perhaps even purchase another home in the future.

After personally experiencing the trauma of foreclosure himself, Anthony has compiled his knowledge and experience into one place—this book—where you can turn for helpful, easy to understand, real–world help should you find yourself in one of these rapidly changing and frustrating situations.

Anthony has made it his purpose in life to help as many people as possible get through and recover financially during these volatile, historic, distressing economic times. This book is a life preserver for those folks drowning in the sea of misfortune that the collapse of the housing bubble brought.

Your finances may be challenging, but let Anthony Biagi and his solid, practical advice guide you back to relative normalcy and on to better, less interesting times.

Best of luck to you.

Garrett Sutton
Attorney, sutlaw.com
Rich Dad Advisor and author

Foreword

Go into any bookstore these days or scroll through any online bookseller and you'll find no shortage of books on self–help that arrive and soon fade from the scene. Nor is there any shortage of books on real estate, finances, investments and retirement plans. This new book by Anthony Biagi, The Homeowner Blueprint: Navigating the Real Estate Storm is one of those rare books that combine both real estate and financial advice as well as a host of suggestions that are as comforting as grandma's homemade chicken soup.

These past few years have devastated the lives of individuals and institutions alike: people out of work, people being forced into bankruptcy, shattered marriages, shattered lives, lost retirement savings. Anthony's book is both personal and objective. He understands that homeowners today who are faced with potential foreclosure or who simply want out from under their current mortgages need honest straightforward answers. This book offers those answers.

No two people's situations are the same. For some, financial duress is the final blow to an unhappy marriage as the strains of paying the bills are just too much for the marriage to bear. Others who want to move to a new city and start a new life find they can't because the home they live in is worth less than what they owe. Savings have vanished. Credit has been destroyed. And minds are so cluttered with fear that they can't seem to make a decision…any decision.

Anthony's book provides a step–by–step manual that will help readers objectively identify the causes of their current financial situation while providing various solutions that can help. From learning how to construct a simple balance sheet to forecasting future scenarios, this book is a true sigh of relief for the homeowner, battered by potential scams, phone calls, and certified letters.

Sit back, take notes, and read this book from cover to cover. It will open your eyes, put a smile on your face, and put your mind at ease. Sometimes just knowing the options is enough. And Anthony provides enough information to strategically take you to safer ground.

Raymond Aaron
New York Times Bestselling Author
UltimateAuthorBootcamp.com

A Note from the Author

The aspiration of home ownership has been a keystone in American society for many years. We are taught that The American Dream is not complete without a home of one's own. Realtor® promote the benefits of home ownership. Government programs encourage people to buy homes through special incentives such as property tax deductions and mortgage interest deductions. There are even special programs for first time homebuyers.

Fannie Mae was created as part of Franklin Delano Roosevelt's New Deal in 1938 Freddie Mac was formed in 1970 to compete with Fannie Mae. The formation of Fannie Mae and Freddie Mac were intended to spur home ownership by buying mortgages from lenders. Once the lenders sold the mortgages to Fannie or Freddie, the lenders could make even more loans. The end of the twentieth century to the beginning of the twenty first century, the 1990s through 2007, were dedicated to increasing home ownership.

When a consumer buys a home all sorts of economic activity takes place. A homeowner will usually pack up all their belongings, and in so doing they get rid of many old items (some to charity, some to friends, some in garage sales, some just hauled away). Often, they will hire a moving van to move their belongings into the new home. From industrious college students to large chains, movers stay in business. Fleets of trucks are bought and serviced. Fuel is purchased. Supplies are needed. Taxes are paid.

Depending on the condition of the home, the happy new homeowner might run down to the carpet store and pick out new carpet. This keeps the carpet companies in business and allows a carpet company to hire workers to deliver and install their carpet. Those carpet layers and movers will take their paychecks and buy other items from still other businesses. Maybe the new home will need new appliances, and so the proud new homeowners go to the appliance store and buy new appliances. While they are at it, they may decide to remodel the entire kitchen of their new home. They hire a general contractor to build a sparkling brand new kitchen. The contractor will need to hire workers to tear out the old kitchen and build a new one. The construction workers take their paychecks and buy other items from still other businesses…okay, you get the picture. From lumber to post–it notes, each business will need supplies. Each business will have to pay to ship those supplies. Each business will pay taxes. Every home bought is like a pebble thrown into the huge financial pond that is the economy of this country.

Home ownership does indeed foster economic growth. It has for decades and will continue to do so. However, something happened at the beginning of this century that had never happened before on such a large scale: Lenders made loans to people who could not repay them.

Prior to 2000, most banks made loans to borrowers that could prove they could qualify for the homes they wanted to purchase. When someone applied for a home loan, the bank required them to provide copies of their recent bank statements, proof of employment, and how much money they made. The banker would then determine if the borrowers could afford the new loan. Those who could were deemed worthy and labeled as having good credit; their loans were approved quickly and painlessly.

For borrowers with damaged credit, there were alternatives available called sub–prime loans. These loans, issued to those whose credit ratings were below "prime," provided borrowers with a mortgage loan for a house while they re–established their credit. Although sub–prime mortgages did in fact have higher rates than those reserved for those with good credit, they still provided an alternative to loan rejection.

Sub–prime lenders still required proof of income and assets from perspective homebuyers. However, they often sold the idea of building credit in the next few years while paying down the initial sub–prime mortgage to these buyers.

The borrower's strategy was to get in the home and refinance the sub–prime loan at a better rate. The idea being that their credit would improve in the future with consistent mortgage and other payments.

New mortgage lenders began to enter the market with full force. These lenders issued mortgage loans at a higher interest rate not only for those with damaged credit, but for those who would not or could not provide proof of income or enough money to close on the new home. These types of loans would have been flatly denied just a few years previously; before the loosened credit requirements brought about by the sub–prime mortgage boom entered the market.

At the same time these new lenders arrived on the scene, money became relatively cheap when compared to previous decades. Not only was it cheap, but it was also easy to get in the form of home loans. Easy money meant nearly everyone who wanted to could buy real estate. As the demand for mortgage–backed securities (i.e., sub–prime loans) increased on Wall Street, the availability of sub–prime mortgages increased. As banks relaxed their lending guidelines, the production of new loans increased and homeowners that previously did not qualify for a home loan were allowed to use adjustable rate mortgages and specialty loans to buy homes. Often the mortgage payments stretched their budgets passed affordability despite "qualifying" for a loan. This created more demand for funds and more demand for real estate. This demand increased home prices at previously unseen levels.

Consumers could buy a home for $350,000 then sell that same home a few months later for $400,000, pocketing a clean $50,000 for nothing more than showing up at the closing table. This speculation caught on. New developments began cropping up with builders offering cheap, easy money. Bidding wars could be found with buyers snapping up new homes as they came on the market and flipping them a few months later to still more eager buyers.

Homes could be bought and sold three to four times within a 12–month period, with each seller making a tidy profit. The eager buyers also knew that they were just a few months away from making their own easy profit on the resale of the home.

It was a real estate merry–go–round. People were encouraged to buy real estate because, if they did not, they would lose out. However, a few years into the new millennium, the merry–go–round began to slow...then it stopped…then it turned around to run in the opposite direction.

People who bought property soon found that the previously insatiable demand for homes began to cool. That meant they would soon have to make mortgage payments that they could not afford. After a few missed mortgage payments, many homeowners had to walk away from their dream home, or they were forced out of their homes by foreclosure.

As more homes began to slide into foreclosure home values dropped. Not just a little, but a lot. People were not buying homes any longer. A home that had previously sold for $500,000, and others like it, were now being listed for as low as $250,000, for example, and remained unsold for months on end.

The lenders and mortgage brokers who made the loans that contributed to this catastrophe are long gone out of business. Sub–prime mortgage loans are also long gone. Loan programs that do not require any documentation are not only now non–existent they are against the law. Borrowers who scammed the system sold their homes, made their money, and moved on.

Now what remains are the good guys…the homeowners who played by the rules and own homes worth less than what they paid for them. These good guys find themselves "upside down" in their homes with mortgage balances exceeding their home values. In the past, if someone got in trouble with their mortgage they could always sell…at least that was the advice given to those who took out sub–prime loans. Everyone knew real estate always went up in value. Just like everyone once knew the earth was flat. People with sub–prime mortgages felt safe because they had the safety net of being able to sell their homes.

Nevertheless, people soon found themselves in homes with no equity in them. If someone was upside down and wanted to sell, they had to bring thousands of dollars to the closing table to satisfy the mortgage company.

Many homeowners today want to get out from under their homes, but they cannot. Well at least do not think they can. This book, *The Homeowner Blueprint: Navigating the Foreclosure Storm* will introduce ways to help those who are currently underwater on their mortgage, under threat of foreclosure, or most importantly…both.

I thank you for picking up this book. Let's weather your storm together. We can do it. Let me teach you how.

*—**Anthony Biagi**, June 2013*

HelpwithHouses.com
Local: 775-393-9478
Toll Free: 855-435-7969
E-mail: Info@helpwithhouses.com
Twitter: @HelpwithHouses
Facebook: https://www.facebook.com/HelpWithHouses
https://www.facebook.com/pages/The-Homeowner-Blueprint-Navigating-the-Real-Estate-Storm/365460893557362
Linkedin: http://www.linkedin.com/pub/anthony-biagi/50/994/988
YouTube Channel: http://www.youtube.com/channel/UCZfJ0odoIoFAP265np7OX9A

Chapter One

The Real Estate Bubble and Crash How Did This Happen?

Who sees with equal eye, as God of all,
A hero perish, or a sparrow fall,
Atoms or systems into ruin hurl'd,
And now a bubble burst, and now a world.

—Alexander Pope, *An Essay on Man: Epistle I*

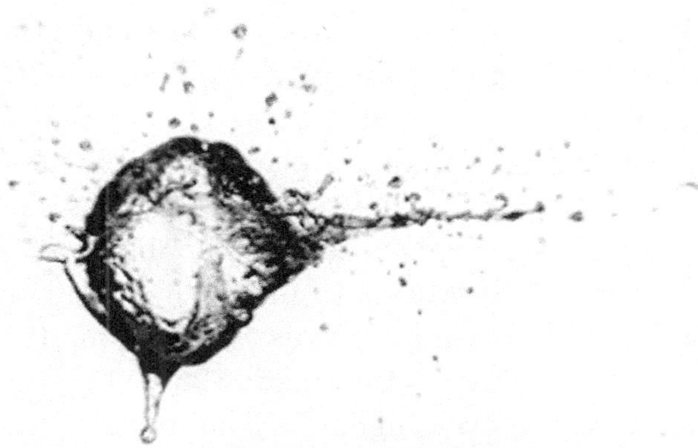

In the interest of simplicity, the sub–prime mortgage rise and collapse can be thought of metaphorically as "putting all your eggs in one basket." And that basket was full of mortgages. When the mortgage basket collapsed, all the economic eggs spilled out and smashed on the ground and the resulting global splatter touched nearly everyone, both locally and globally. This upheaval in the market ignited the recession in dramatic fashion in September 2008.

How did this happen? Well, it was due to a number of factors. Let's go through them chronologically, and I'll explain how each factor contributed to the eventual destruction of the housing market. I will explain how a house of straw, with no foundation, became a pile of debris that eventually blew all over the world with one brisk gust of wind.

Low Interest Rates—Interest rates on home loans fell, to the lowest levels in 40 years, in the early 2000s causing a buying frenzy of homes. The demand for homes increased the price of homes that fed sales like a snake eating its tail.

Real Estate Prices—A continued increase in home prices led to huge leaps and bounds in appraisal values. Everyone wanted a piece of that pie, and the demand increased value, and houses were being sold at record high rates both in quantity and cost.

Sub–Prime Mortgage Loans—Banks and other lenders were extending credit, especially mortgage credit, to buyers with less than perfect credit. In some cases they were lending money to people with terrible credit, or even an inability to verify income.

Liar Loans—Loans given to those unable to prove their income, such as self–employed people, in which case, no supportive documents or other information was required for the loan approval. One could ostensibly say they made $250,000, get a loan for a home in that amount or even higher, and not have to verify their income.

ARM—Adjustable Rate Mortgage. In theory, an ARM adjusts with the market and interest rates. If rates fall after an ARM originates, it will adjust down when it reaches its recast date. If rates rise after the ARM origination then it will adjust up when it recasts. The hope was that sub–prime borrowers would finance with ARMs, pay their notes on time to improve their credit score, which would allow them to finance with more traditional, fixed–

rate loan products after their credit improved or recovered. ARMs have one, three, five, or seven year fixed entry periods, so there was a mortgage product with a timeline that could help every homeowner, even sub–prime borrowers, afford to buy their piece of the American Dream. This would, therefore, keep their payments low, and their ability to afford their home. Unfortunately, for most homebuyers during this time, the ARM adjusted upward, and some homeowners saw their monthly mortgage payments double or triple. In the meantime, their wages stayed the same. They simply could not afford the new payments and many drained savings accounts, defaulted on loans, and some lost their homes to foreclosure.

Home Equity Loans—With the prices of real estate jumping so dramatically and quickly—I know a man who bought a house three months before his wedding, and by his wedding day, the house had already increased in price by $20,000; everyone wanted in on the dream real estate market. People all over were taking out equity loans on their homes. They were able to leverage the increased value of their house over and above what they had paid for it since it was worth more due to rapid appreciation. Many made major home upgrades, or took luxury vacations, or bought new cars, boats, jet skis, or other things they generally would not buy, because they could not normally afford them. But suddenly, now, it was a reality. The alluring appeal of real estate always hovered in the back of one's mind because "Real estate only increases in value...right?"

Asset Backed Securities —Mortgages packaged into bundles and then sold to investors, with the property, in this case houses, as collateral. They were packaged and re–sold to hedge funds, pension funds, and international governments.

Originated Mortgages—It became very profitable to fund mortgages, even to those without verified income and/or no down payment. Some loans were underwritten for 125 percent of the price of the home because the value of real estate was increasing so quickly. Buyers could use that extra 25 percent as a down payment on the property, or to buy new furniture, re–do the kitchen, and so on.

Credit Ratings—Many investors relied on professional credit raters such as the Government National Mortgage Association, (Ginnie Mae, a corporation within the US Government's Department of Housing and Urban Development, aka HUD.), and other stable and long–lived firms like Standard and Poor's who gave AAA credit ratings to packaged mortgage securities the highest investor safety rating. It is both interesting and important to note that the U.S. government is taking legal action against many credit rating organizations for fraud.

Mortgage Backed Securities (or MBS)—Mortgages which were packaged together with other loans, then sold and traded on Wall Street as packages of loans to investors who traditionally did not invest in home loans and mortgages.

The market crash was precipitated by the stalling and then falling of home prices and the increasing number of homeowners who were defaulting on their mortgages. In traditional debt–holding circles, non–payment on mortgages went straight to foreclosure. There were no workout, no refinancing, no loan modifications, and no mortgage debt relief programs available at that time. Default rates began rising at such a percentage that the packaged mortgaged backed securities became less profitable, and many investors shied away from purchasing them. Other investment strategies became popular and then they, too, began plummeting in value. Nervous lenders began calling in debts, and banks that were neck–deep in collateral loans found they had no actual liquid capital and began going out of business. It seemed as if everyone who had invested in MBSs and CBOs (collateral backed obligations, similar to a MBS), suddenly found they were holding not investments but paper that was worth far less than what they paid for it. In essence, their investments were now worth almost nothing.

Unfortunately, this spiraling out of control of both the real estate and banking industries rippled outward, causing cut–backs and layoffs in every category of business. People who were current on their mortgages suddenly found themselves unable to make the payments after losing their job, and then they, too, were in foreclosure. All of this only added to the already massive mountain of foreclosed properties. The U.S. and other global economies have still not recovered from this vicious cycle.

This is an oversimplification of a very complex problem, but essentially, this is how the housing bubble collapsed and nearly took down everyone who had invested in it around the world.

A More Detailed Explanation

It is important to note, and to be a little more technical mapping out just what happened when the housing bubble burst. The systemic collapse of the housing market had little to do with the individual and more to do with big banks and Wall Street. They had constructed a house of cards (pun absolutely intended), which the economy and families were balancing on, and eventually, as it had to, that house fell. It was, and still is, a very scary time to be a homeowner.

Let's take a look back in time to understand where we are now. From the late 1990s through 2006, I watched as the price of middle–class American real estate increased by on average 55 percent (US Census Bureau, 2013). During this time, credit was extremely easy to get for financing new home loans and new homeowners. During this time, many people became first time homebuyers. The homeowners that owned homes during this time often financed consumer debt through a cash–out refinance transaction or home equity lines of credit to pay off consumer credit lines. The new loans had more agreeable terms regarding payment so consumers began taking their credit card debt and car payments and refinancing them by adding them to the house payment. Generally the interest rate on a home loan is much lower than the interest rates being charged on their other lines of credit such as credit cards, so consumers found themselves paying less overall in interest charges. This system was loaded with a spring or a trigger, however, because the debt was secured by the value of the house, not just the credit worthiness of the homeowners themselves. You can see how this easily led to people spending more than their credit worthiness would allow. People in appreciating house value zones were now able to have inexpensive credit because their house value went up...at times over 100 percent (The National Center for Policy Analysis, 2011) in less than a decade. This was roughly from 1997 up through 2006. It's important to recognize that various local markets reacted differently to the change in credit liquidity and value of real estate.

With the market value of homes dropping quickly in the real estate market starting in the middle of 2006, it did not take long to fall 20 percent by the end of 2008. Homeowners that decided to finance with an adjustable rate mortgage that had a fixed term ending in 2006–2008 suddenly saw a tighter market for home financing. They could not have known that from 2000 through 2003 that their loan would "re–cast," or return to market rates and calculate the new payment at the new market interest rate, in the midst of a credit crisis. Neither students nor future homeowners in the U.S. are taught real estate cycles and interest rate cycles, and the outcome of this lack of financial training was that the average American homebuyer definitely was not prepared for the worst. Many were told at the time of refinancing that this was the only type of mortgage they qualified for and without this loan, they would not get the keys to their new home. Mortgage professionals often sold loans to new home buyers that had adjustable rate loan programs set to re–cast three to seven years later. They sold these loans telling buyers that this was their only option given their credit worthiness. That years later, when the loan was about to recast, they would be able to finance with a more permanent loan. It was understood that this was only possible after they demonstrated credit worthiness with the improved credit created by three to seven years of mortgage payments. Some homeowners improved their credit, while others found a credit crisis that did not allow them to refinance like the mortgage professional implied.

These loans had low "teaser–rates" that were fixed for a period of one year to 10 years depending on the loan program, with most being in the three to seven year fixed term timeline. Without a financial education and absolutely no understanding as to how these loans compensated mortgage brokers and investment bankers to sell them, it was very difficult for many homeowners to make the best financial decision for their situation. That is, without understanding that certain adjustable rate mortgage programs paid mortgage brokers, loan officers and banks a higher return on their time spent with homeowners than a plain vanilla fixed rate loan that compensated the mortgage professionals less, homeowners did not always make the soundest financial decision they could have. Many made the most inexpensive decision for now and paid for it handsomely later. Most loans offered low entry interest rates for a period of years and adjusted to market rates based on various indices at a later date. Homeowners that waited to refinance their homes when the fixed entry period was up had to refinance in the given market they found themselves in, and many found themselves in a market where their home value was declining for the first time since they purchased it. With declining home values the borrowers that financed at the top of the market were already finding themselves underwater and over–financed. Changes to income or other financial hardships compounded homeowners' problems and made it more difficult to finance under new stricter underwriting guidelines after the bubble burst, home values plummeted and loan qualification became more difficult.

In 2007, the first full year with property values in decline, mortgage lenders opened foreclosure proceedings on 1.3 million files or 79 percent more than the 2006 total. Through 2008, foreclosure filings increased to 2.3 million properties for an 81 percent increase over 2007. By the end of 2008, 9.2 percent of mortgaged homes were delinquent or already in foreclosure. That is one or more on every block in the country.

It is difficult to get official updated numbers, but there were expected to be as many as 9 million houses in foreclosure between 2009 and 2011. In March 2009, lenders executed 341,180 foreclosures. For the three-year period, it is estimated that 3 million homeowners lost their homes to foreclosure annually. Numbers report up to 2.7 million in any one calendar year, with some rolling 12 month averages over 3 million at the foreclosure peak. Exactly when that peak happened or will happen has yet to be seen with enough market data to determine. Even if the bottom of the market in real estate values were actually already hit, the foreclosure rate would cycle behind that by some time since there would be no understanding of the market bottom until years later when people start debating it. Only the future will know if these cycles are true or false bottoms.

In short, there are many things that happened on scales at which they had never happened before during this mortgage meltdown and crisis. There was a drive to deregulate the mortgage lending industry that allowed the sub–prime mortgage market to skyrocket and originate many loans to less credit worthy borrowers. This relaxed credit cycle allowed for a housing boom that saw many new homes built very rapidly as well as older homes being remodeled and returned to the lending market at higher appraisal values. With prices increasing, due to rising demand for new homes, relaxed credit for sub–prime borrowers, and an increased appetite from Wall Street for more mortgage–backed securities there was a perfect storm pushing prices ever higher. All while sub–prime credit made it seem like people in the market could afford it all while Wall Street would accept any loan package that was stamped AAA, because they already had a buyer or bidding war waiting for the bundle.

This was all not possible without the cooperation of the other parts of the lending and finance world. There were underwriters stamping securitized loan packages as AAA when they included sub–prime mortgages, underwritten by yet further underwriters, with stated or no income verification and little reserve asset requirements. There were underwriters writing insurance policies to the banks and finance houses that brokered the securitized investments on Wall Street. There were underwriters in the broker houses writing final documents on loan packages sold to foreign investors, pension funds, other hedge funds and large banking institutions.

They came about due to these relaxed practices of the financial underwriting and insurance underwriting across many portions of the financial industry caused the systemic collapse that nearly brought the financial system as a whole to its knees. The need for greater volume of a very lucrative financial instrument caused the whole system to relax its regulations and allow more to happen faster. A foreclosure storm that kicked off with well over 50 percent of banks and lending institutions closing their doors at the bubble's peak and soon after when money dried up and many banks lost their charter, came about due to these relaxed practices.

There is a great deal of evidence piling up that those who were involved in mortgage lending were both perpetrators and victims of fraud. One blogger, Ian Welsh at his blog of the same name, on June 26, 2010 went so far as to say that half of the loans packaged during the housing bubble were fraudulent, and which contributed to the housing bubble crash.

An Important Tool for Your Foreclosure Toolkit: What you need to know now.

There is a new issue, now, in that some, maybe even many, of these loans were packaged as securities to be traded on Wall Street. They were then re–packaged, and sold again, repeatedly, to the point that banks no longer have the original loan paperwork, including the promissory note that is needed to foreclose on a property. Perhaps incredibly, no one seems to know where they are. Research varies on how many promissory notes are missing, but saying that at least half of all promissory notes from the sub–prime housing boom are missing would not be unreasonable.

Additionally, if one looks further into the mortgage backed security issue, you will find that in order to become an asset–backed security, there cannot be a promissory note attached to the security. What this means is that in order to create packages of loans to sell as a group, the promissory notes were destroyed. This was required since any asset traded on Wall Street cannot legally be foreclosed on by anyone other than the owner of the asset. Since the assets were packaged and sold in an instrument that allowed them to be traded and resold, they were no longer foreclosable notes originated and controlled by the original lender. In order for many loans to be foreclosed on, there will be a need for some previously destroyed promissory notes to magically reappear (Time Magazine, 2010). The reason it is important to have the promissory note to initiate and process a foreclosure is because of:

Article 3 of the Uniform Commercial Code, which states:

The Uniform Commercial Code forbids foreclosure of the mortgage unless the creditor possesses the properly negotiated original promissory note. If this cannot be done, the foreclosure must stop.

This rule is valid in every jurisdiction in the United States (with a minor variation in New York). If the mortgage originator, who historically has held the original promissory note at its location, such as a bank, cannot provide the original signed promissory note, by law, the foreclosure cannot move forward. If you are in foreclosure, you may be able to stop the process until such time that the promissory note can be produced. This can take anywhere from weeks to months, but it will buy you some time. You will need to file a counterclaim with the court, and do so quickly. My suggestion would be to hire an attorney to fight this battle for you as the issue is a complex one. Additionally, you only have 20–30 days to respond to a foreclosure complaint (in judicial states; non–judicial states vary by state. (Visit the following website to determine if you live in a judicial or non-judicial state: http://www.realtytrac.com/foreclosure-laws/foreclosure-laws-comparison.asp). Remember, you must act quickly!

Make sure you choose someone reputable. If you do hire an attorney, you can check their status with the bar association in your state or county or both, usually online at no charge. The Bar Association in your area may also be able to offer you a free consultation with an attorney, so do not hesitate to call them. Do everything you can except hesitate. A notice of foreclosure is a time for action.

If you cannot afford an attorney, many communities with law schools have students at the law school who give free advice (under supervision); you can also check to see if there is a legal aid office in your community. If you have a government loan such as

Freddie Mac, a HUD office may be able to assist you. You have options, but you must act fast.

Lastly, although there are steps in place to re-create lost or misplaced promissory notes under subsection 3–309 of the Uniform Commercial Code, the process is lengthy. Significant other evidence must be provided to the court, by the mortgage holder, i.e., lender, in order for the new promissory note to be recognized as valid. In many cases, if you file a counterclaim against the lender who is foreclosing on you, and they cannot provide the original promissory note, yet continue with the foreclosure proceedings, they may be in legal jeopardy of committing fraud under the Truth in Lending Act.

Chapter Two

Navigating the Foreclosure Storm and the Underwater Mortgage

How to Use This Book to Protect Yourself

Home is where the heart is.

—Pliny the Elder

Patti and Jeff

In 2005, Patti and Jeff, a married couple with a two- year-old daughter, decided to buy a house. She had just been promoted to a management position at the big multinational firm she worked at, and her husband's construction business was growing almost faster than he could keep up. They purchased a fixer–upper in a nice area between their work areas for $350,000. Eighteen months later, Jeff had made many repairs and done a lot of remodeling to the home, and they had built up enough equity to sell and trade up for a bigger house in a nicer neighborhood for $650,000.

When the housing bubble burst and the recession hit, Jeff found his construction jobs drying up. He went from making $10,000 a month to $0 per month. They were trying to survive on Patti's manager salary alone. In the meantime, their family had expanded to four with the birth of a son. By 2009, the house was underwater. They had paid $650,000 for it in 2006, and now it was worth half that, yet their payments remained the same. Patti, Jeff and their children were in trouble.

***

Home sweet home. It's the American dream. Every man and woman wants that castle. If you bought a home in the last ten years and are reading this book, it's likely you are facing some serious financial problems. Either that or you think you may soon. If you think back to the mortgage approval process when you first bought your home you can no doubt recall all the thinking that went into your decision to buy a home. Your thoughts probably included some of the following:

- Maybe you weren't exactly ready, but the market made it a good time to buy.
- Maybe your friends bought a new home and that spurred your thinking about it.
- Maybe your family was growing and you needed more space.

- Perhaps you simply wanted to move into a new neighborhood.

- Or, like Patti, Jeff, and others like them, in the early to mid 2000s, it was just too easy to be approved for a loan.

So you did a little looking on the web and began to search for homes in the area you were considering moving. You looked at a few houses and began to get a little excited. After a week or two of viewing homes online, you decided that it was time to get a bit more serious and call a real estate agent to look at some homes in person.

Once you found a home you liked, you began the mortgage application process. Within a matter of a few of days, you were likely buried in paperwork. New terms were thrown at you—terms like "impounds" and "annual percentage rate." You were supposed to review those loan disclosures, sign them and initial them, assuring the lender you understood them—whether you did or not—because you knew your loan wouldn't move forward without the myriad scattering of initials and signatures.

You didn't want anything to slow down the process, because of what was waiting for you at the end of all that paperwork: your new home. That is what you were focusing on. The paperwork was just a hassle to get through so you could move in. Besides, you trusted your loan officer, your bank, even the government. Surely, there was oversight all along the way to keep you from getting into too much trouble. Wasn't that what all the paperwork you signed was about? Wasn't that the reason it was all so complicated? Wasn't that why you were giving so much money to all those people who were supposedly experts?

Is this scenario a familiar one to you?

It's natural to feel a little overwhelmed by the onslaught of new information that comes with buying a home. Most of us don't get any kind of financial education in school, and the terminology, what is generally called "jargon," can be as daunting as any foreign language. The Merriam Webster online dictionary describes jargon as a: *noun: (2) the technical terminology or characteristic idiom of a special activity or group.* And every industry has its own. When you bought your house you probably encountered a whole lot of words and phrases you probably never heard before. What is routine to a mortgage loan officer is anything but commonplace to a consumer.

You can probably remember going through all those hoops like it was yesterday. You answered this, and then answered that. Signed this, and then signed that. Delivered this, and then faxed that...all for the sole purpose of getting a home loan you were told would be a piece of cake. You ended up exhausted as well as bewildered. You asked yourself: *What have I signed up for? What have I agreed to? Will someone eventually explain it to me?* You not only felt abused but abandoned. No one could fully answer your questions—or if they could, they didn't. There seemed nowhere to turn for real answers; everyone was trying to sell you something or make money from your transaction. All you wanted to do was buy that house!

So you signed, and signed, and signed. Eventually, someone handed you a set of keys and you moved in and began making mortgage payments on your new home! You were so proud and excited. Maybe you even took out an equity loan for home improvements within a few years of purchasing. But then...

Something went wrong. Despite decades of everyone thinking real estate would always go up in value, it started to drop...and it kept dropping. It dropped across the country. Put simply, in mid–2007, the housing bubble burst.

It wasn't just you. As you can see in Figure 1, home prices fell, on average, $72,000 over three years, although in some states that number was as high as 50 percent below the 2007 average price. Those houses lost *half* their value in *three* years—through no fault of the homeowners.

You and your family are not in this alone: thousands and thousands of people have been affected by the housing collapse. It hit this country like a ton of bricks, and we are all still digging out from the rubble. It wasn't anything you did.

Figure 1. Average U.S. Home Prices 2000 to 2012. Data compiled april 2013 from http://www.census.gov/const/uspriceann.pdf and http://ycharts.com/indicators/sales_price_of_existing_homes

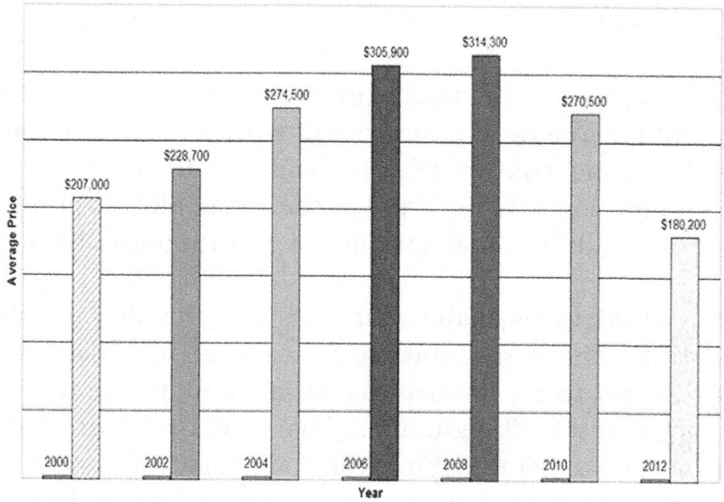

In the first quarter of 2009, in the state of Nevada for example, home foreclosure filings were up 111 percent from the first quarter of 2008 (Trulia.com, 2009). Arizona, California, Florida, and Illinois were close behind.

How and why the collapse happened isn't as important as getting out of the bad situation you may be facing today. We can learn from the past, but we can't change it. What we can change is what happens *now.*

If you're facing foreclosure or you're underwater on your mortgage (don't worry; I'll explain potentially unfamiliar terms shortly), you might share some similar experiences with Patti and Jeff or other homeowners in the same circumstances. Suddenly, you get letters in the mail with terms you don't clearly understand. Postcards arrive from people you've never met, all wanting to "help" you. Banks have all the 30, 60, 90 days late information for their accounts, and when they are not paid it's time to get in touch with you. Investors will send letters when issued a notice of default. Your phone never stops ringing from people or organizations you've never heard of because there are list sources that create alerts when a debtor passes or approaches one of those 30, 60 and 90 days late deadlines. These go out to your mortgage holders and to others, some of who are looking to exploit your situation. That's one of the main reasons I wrote this book: I want to help as many people as I can before they reach the point of no return.

Now you're in a situation that is even more strange, frightening, and unfamiliar. You're in a new world with new jargon and new experts. This time what waits at the end of it all is nothing as exciting as a new home. What waits at the end of all this paperwork feels like a long drop into a dark abyss. But it doesn't have to be.

I wrote this book to help calm your fears and provide you with different options. These are solutions that people just like you have used in the past to get themselves out of similar situations. This isn't theory, and it isn't a gimmick. This book isn't part of a seminar, an investment club asking you for money, or a sales pitch. This is good, solid information gleaned from my years in the real estate and mortgage business, and designed to help you, the average homeowner help yourself. It's filled with what I have seen work for the people I have helped. I designed this book with regular people, like Patti and Jeff, in mind. The words in this book represent homes retained, credit scores redeemed, marriages saved, dreams kept on course. I don't care if that sounds presumptive or grandiose to some people. We're talking about people's *homes* here. It doesn't get much bigger than that. I know what I'm talking about—I lived through it, too.

This book was designed to provide immediate answers and assistance. Throughout these chapters are tools, presented in layman's terms, regarding exactly what's going on in your current mortgage situation and to:

1. Identify how you got into your situation;
2. Form a strategy for how you can get out of it.

My advice is based upon tried and true principles. These are not general theories or "secrets" that might be seen on TV or the Internet and promise to solve all your problems easily and quickly. If it sounds too good to be true, it probably is.

What I'd like to do, and this is based on my years of experience in real estate, is to have this book guide you, not *tell* you what to do. Every situation is a little different. Everyone has found their way to where they are by taking different paths. That means one answer isn't going to be the correct answer for everyone. In this book, you will find examples of those who have been in situations similar to yours and how they arrived at their solutions.

Before you find a solution, however, you need to determine the problem. Let's first look at some terminology, get some explanations on what these words mean and their impact on your choices, your credit, and your future.

Three terms need explaining at the outset:

- Pre–foreclosure;
- Foreclosure;
- Underwater.

Figure 2. Foreclosure Increase, by Percentage and State, Third Quarter of 2008 vs. Third Quarter of 2009, Data compiled from realtytrac.com/foreclosure/foreclosure-rates.html, accessed March 2013.

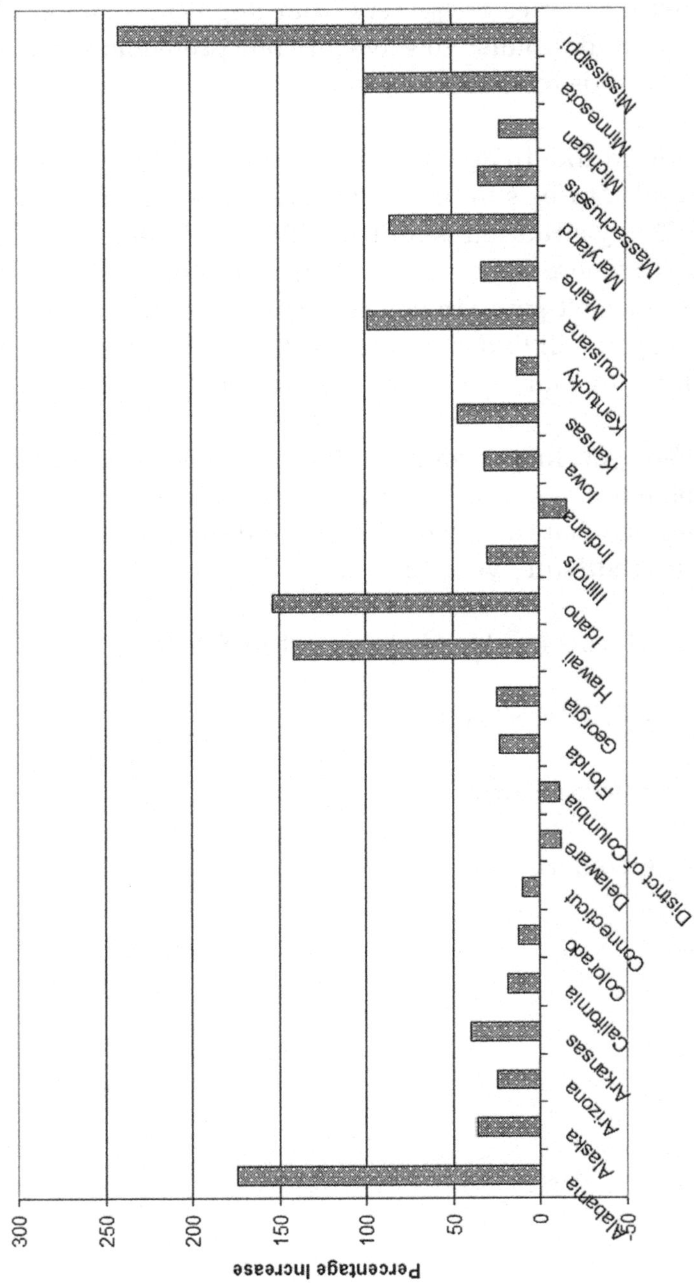

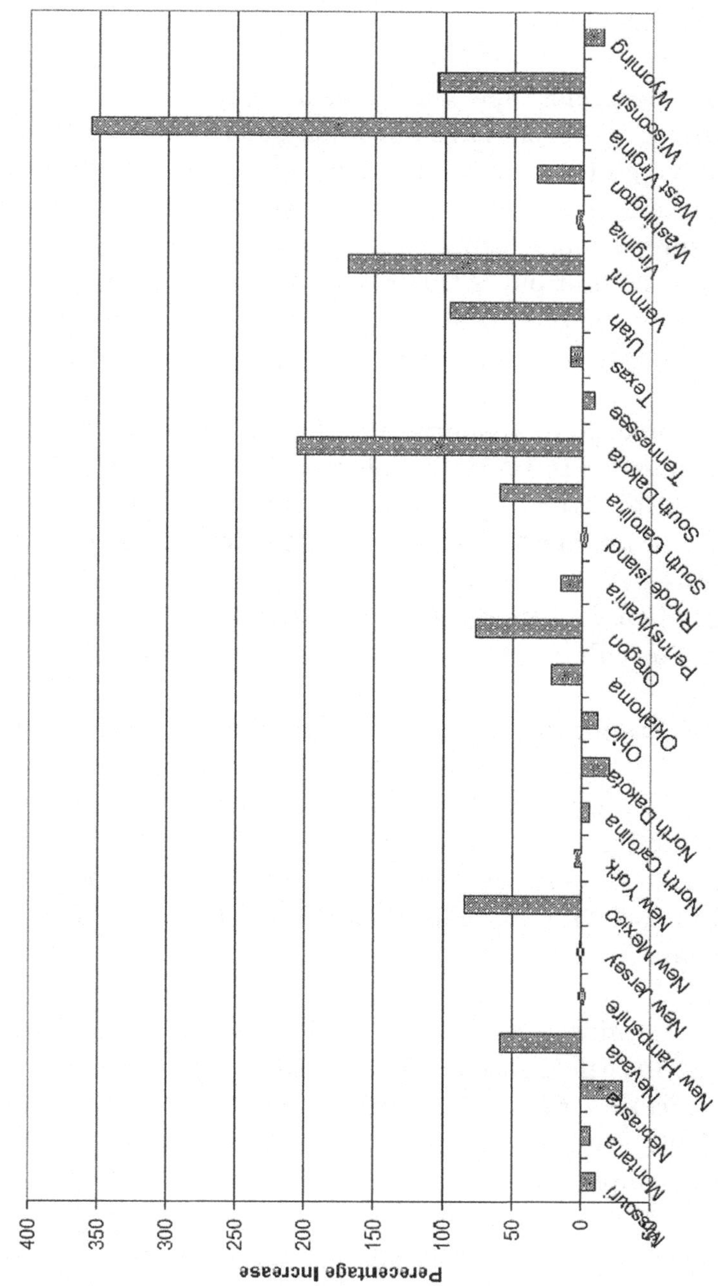

Figure 2.1. Foreclosure Increases, by Percentage, Third Quarter of 2008 vs. Third Quarter of 2009, Data compiled from realtytrac.com/foreclosure/foreclosure-rates.html, accessed March 2013.

Let's begin with:

Pre–Foreclosure

Lenders cannot take your home away from you on a whim. Home ownership is sacred in this country, and rightly so. When someone is having difficulty paying their mortgage, or soon will be, mortgage companies have to take specific, predetermined steps when considering foreclosing on a property. A pre–foreclosure is a trigger event that paves the way for the legal process of a bank taking back the collateral for a mortgage. If that mortgage is yours, that collateral is *your home*.

Pre–foreclosure, essentially, happens when you miss your mortgage payments, typically in increments of three to six months in a row. At that time, you, as well as any additional signers, if any, of the original mortgage will be notified by the lender(s) of past–due status by a certified letter. This means that if someone else co–signed on your mortgage, such as your parents or other relative, they too will get the same certified notification.

This pre–foreclosure letter is the formal notice that the bank intends to foreclose because you are behind on your payments. Typically, you have 90 days to resolve the shortage and come up to date on your payments. This does vary by state. In judicial states a *lis pendens (*e.g., suit pending), is issued at the 90–day late mark. In non–judicial states a notice of default is issued at 90 days late.

To determine if you live in a judicial or non–judicial state, simply do an Internet search using the following search phrase: *How can I determine if I live in a judicial or non–judicial state?* Visit this website: http://www.realtytrac.com/foreclosure-laws/foreclosure-laws-comparison.asp.

The original loan documents you signed when you purchased the property (or if you refinanced the loan, then on that date) contained language about the lender's rights. The pre–foreclosure letter will spell out what might happen should you not become current with your monthly payments, how much you have to pay, and the last date that the payment can be made in order to avoid foreclosure.

From 2007 to 2011, home foreclosures nearly doubled. In some states, it was even higher than that; however, we're starting to see these numbers come back down (Figure 3).

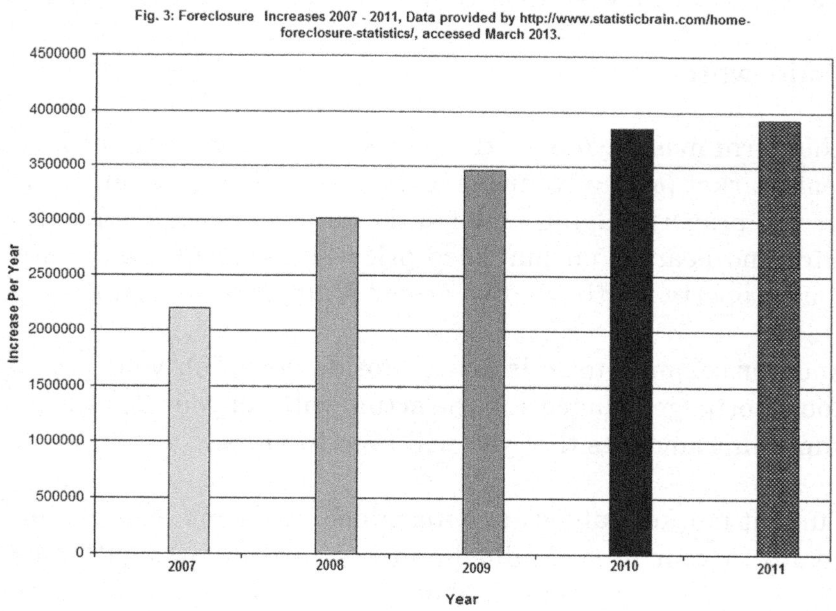

Foreclosure

If you do not catch up with your overdue payments and you skip the next payment after the time allotted in the pre–foreclosure document, the bank can, and probably will, foreclose on you. You and all parties that are on the mortgage note will be notified that the property is in foreclosure. This information will come to you in the form of another certified letter, and again will be sent to all co–signers of the original mortgage.

In this letter, you will be given the amount needed to stop the foreclosure process, what is called the "reinstatement" amount (which includes past due mortgage payments), the current mortgage payment due, and all legal fees accrued. If you cannot pay the reinstatement amount or work out a plan with the lender, your home will go to foreclosure, the home will be sold to a third party or kept by the lender, and you will be evicted from your home. The foreclosure process is then completed.

But wait! Don't panic! Foreclosure is the bank's last option, and you have a few options to consider before it gets to that point.

Underwater

This term means your mortgage balance is higher than the current market price of your home. It doesn't matter what you paid for the property. Being underwater on your mortgage has absolutely no bearing on purchase price—it is about value only. Is your property worth what you owe? If not, it is underwater.

Another common term is being "upside down" on your property. Your mortgage balance and the actual value of your home are two important amounts that you will need to know.

Current market values are determined by recent sales of similar homes in your area. Trained and licensed professional appraisers will go out to your neighborhood and make a determination on your home's value based on several factors, the first being, of course, your house itself. The next important measuring stick they will use is a recent sale, or "comp" for "comparable", to a home that has sold within the previous six to twelve months in your area. It will also have similar characteristics to your home including the number of bedrooms, bathrooms, square footage, amenities such as a pool, and so forth.

In this example, Patti and Jeff purchased their home five years ago for $650,000 and took out a mortgage loan for $530,000. Today, however, two homes in their neighborhood, one slightly larger and one slightly smaller, have both sold, one at $270,000 and the other at $255,000. It is likely their home is worth somewhere between these two amounts given similar age, condition of the home, and any improvements made to the property. Since receiving their 30–year mortgage, they have lowered it to around $490,000 by making their payments of $3349.96 to principal and interest. Their total payment with tax ($500/mo) and insurance ($150/mo) impounds included, was approximately $4,000. With Jeff's $10,000 monthly income and Patti's $80,000 annual manager's salary, their $200,000 annual income was loosely verified when qualifying for the loan, because they had good credit, they had a 20 percent down payment in cash from the sale of their other house, so they were golden the day they bought the house. After paying on their mortgage for 6 years, their balance was about $490,000 with their value in the $255,000 to $270,000 range when looking at recent comparable sales.

Homeowners are often surprised how little their mortgage balance has dropped during the early years of a mortgage. This is because most people don't understand how mortgage amortization works: the bulk of mortgage interest is paid near the front of the loan and the bulk of the principal balance is paid near the end of the loan.

Here is an additional example showing a mortgage that is underwater:

- A home was bought in 1999 for $250,000 with an interest only payment and a 10–year fixed interest period;

- The owners made payments of $1200 per month for ten years. ($144,000 in interest payments, paying no money to the principal balance);

- In 2009, comps were valued at $120,000, $145,000 and $150,000; the 2009 valuation of their home was $150,000;

- The amount owed on the mortgage is still $250,000 having paid their interest only payment at $1200 monthly just to maintenance the $250,000 balance; the mortgage balance is about $100,000 more than what the home is worth;

• In 2009, if the owners wanted to sell their home at current market prices, they would still owe the lender the $100,000 difference and would need to bring a $100,000 check to the closing table to offset the lender's loss;

• Their options at this point are to explore a short sale or a loan modification. Their home is underwater.

One thing to note here is that having a home underwater and a home in foreclosure don't necessarily go hand in hand. Being underwater does not mean you're also late on your monthly payments. Either situation—being in foreclosure or being underwater—can present some serious financial challenges. While late mortgage payments will damage your credit rating, a foreclosure will cause the ultimate damage.

Foreclosure Fallout

Besides losing your home, your credit history report will take a hard hit, too. This will make it extremely difficult to find an apartment or house to rent—that is, unless you can prove to your new landlord that you had some isolated instances that caused the foreclosure you experienced. If you can show that the circumstances will not happen again, you may have a chance of getting someone to take a gamble on you. But...it will take some work and, in most cases, cause you to pay a higher monthly rent due to your credit score.

A foreclosure will be viewed by a mortgage company as the worst thing that can occur in your credit history, even worse than a bankruptcy. If you are foreclosed upon and re–establish your credit history after a couple of years (which can easily be done), a lender still won't approve you for a new mortgage loan until more than five years have passed since the foreclosure date. This is only if you have been absolutely perfect in repairing your credit, with NOT ONE late payment to anyone.

Bottom line: You don't want a foreclosure.

Something important to consider...if you're foreclosed upon and the lender sells the home for less than the balance of your loan, depending on the nature of your note, the lender can obtain a deficiency judgment against you hoping to recover the remaining balance on your old mortgage...**from you.**

On the other hand, a lender can forgive the old debt. The remaining balance, however, may be charged to you on a future IRS form 1099C. The IRS considers this to be income passed on to you and will expect you to pay income taxes on the forgiven balance.

TAKE NOTE: Through December 31, 2013, you may be eligible for the Mortgage Debt Relief Act. Originally only available through 2012, it has been extended through 2013. You don't want to miss this opportunity. In short, this federal law allows you to exclude forgiven debt from a loan restructuring or foreclosure in cases where the bank writes off the difference between your mortgage amount and the sale amount of the property (and which the IRS considers to be "income") from your tax return. It thereby eliminates the IRS requirement of paying taxes on the forgiven amount. **This can potentially save you thousands of dollars.**

Financial worries and negative credit can affect every single aspect of your life, physically and emotionally. Negative credit can affect your relationships with your family, your co–workers, and anyone in your circle. Numerous psychological studies have determined that anxiety over finances have consistently shown to be one of the highest stressors that can be experienced by an individual or family (NBCNews.com, 2013). Negative reactions to stress can include verbal aggression, which may lead to emotional or physical abuse; relief from stress can manifest through alcohol or drug use, depression, and sadness over the loss of home, property, and lifestyle. Physical manifestations of pain and other ailments are common. Every member of the family is affected.

Negative credit may also restrict your employment opportunities in the future. A growing number of occupations require pre–employment credit checks to determine the trustworthiness and dependability of a candidate.

None of this is good stuff. *Yet, be not afraid. I can help.*

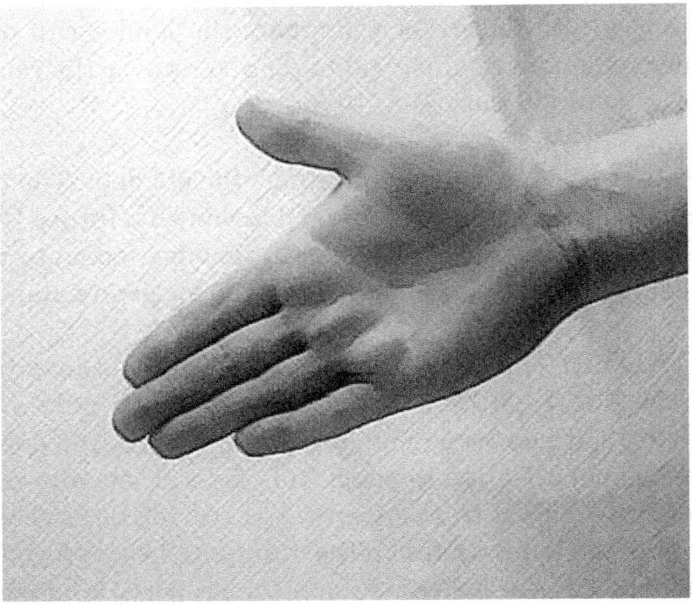

Making any of these choices can be tough. You didn't plan to be where you are today. I understand these situations, and I would like to help. I have made helping people in this situation my mission in life. I've been in the real estate business for a long time. I even found myself in the same position you are right now, but I don't want to get ahead of myself. Let me start from the beginning.

Why I Want To Help

My real life experience overcoming obstacles and discovering my inner courage happened when I was 15-years-old. I was your typical high school teen, and the most important thing in my life was baseball. I wanted to play high school ball, college baseball, and of course, I dreamed of going to the majors.

All of my dreams were abruptly yanked out from under me when I was diagnosed with a desmoid tumor on my right scapula. My world would never be the same. I would shortly discover what radiation treatments were all about. I missed a full year of school, and I would never play baseball at any competitive level again.

Of the twelve of us who entered treatment together for the same type of tumor, I am the only one who has not had a recurrence. I don't know what to attribute this to other than positivity, prayer, and blind luck. That type of hardship, at that age, proved to me that I had what it took to overcome odds, to forge through the bad times, and literally live to come out the other side and get on with life.

This early skirmish with health issues and hospitals would simply toughen my personal resolve and underscore my ability to get through obstacles with determination and character. In many ways, these hardships prepared me for the collapse of the real estate market.

My experience in real estate started when I was 19-years-old. I was attending college, enjoying being young and on my own for the first time. This carefree time came to a halt, abruptly, when my father passed away. A small inheritance came to both my brother and me. I wondered what to do with the money. Then I realized: My dad would want me to do something that was a smart investment—he was an entrepreneur and investor, and here was a way I could emulate him.

I felt I needed to watch out for my family and, with that in mind, I bought my first house. It was a two master–bedroom townhouse. I moved into one bedroom, and rented out the other, and the tenant paid most of my mortgage by paying rent.

Over the next three years, I purchased two more houses. At each new property the tenant covered the mortgage cost of my property by paying rent. By the time I had bought a third house, even when adding in the cost of hiring a property manager, the rent payments of all three properties actually covered my costs while I was in school.

As I became more involved in real estate, and struggled with the passing of my father, I quit UNR (the University of Nevada, Reno) to focus on real estate full time and play a bigger role in my family. I went to work for Academy Mortgage where I learned a lot about mortgages and the mortgage industry—more than I could pick up just doing my own deals. I spent every free moment I had reading books about real estate, taking classes, or attending seminars. I was going to tackle the real estate industry with the same level of determination that I used to fight my serious health conditions and the loss of my father.

Then, in 2006, and because I was so in tune with the housing market, I saw that the real estate bubble was deflating and would likely burst, and soon I left that world for another. In 2007 I moved to Florida to manage an up–and–coming health insurance agency.

While I was managing the healthcare agency in Florida, the housing sector finally collapsed. I was unable to keep my Nevada properties rented, and I fell behind on the mortgage payments. I had difficulty finding anyone to help me, particularly as I was living out of state in Florida. I needed to short sale my properties——and we'll cover short sales later in this book—but I was in unfamiliar territory. I didn't know what to do or who could help.

Finally, I made a business decision: I decided to quit paying on my mortgages, keep the cash, and let the banks foreclose on my properties. I had equity lines in the hundreds of thousands of dollars just months earlier, and suddenly, I had zero. My credit score was negatively affected very quickly—it went from 810 to below 500 almost before I knew what was happening.

That's when I realized there was a need in the real estate industry. People like me needed someone to guide them through the process when they were in foreclosure, underwater, or both.

After learning by living through all the hardships and coming out stronger, I decided I should be that person to fill the gap. I had the background, education, and personal experience necessary to help other people pull together the pieces of their financial lives. Out of that terrible time in my life, *Help With Houses* was born. You don't have to be out there yourself; I'm using my experience to help people just like you benefit from my hard–won knowledge every day.

I helped Patti and Jeff avoid foreclosure and receive of a deficiency judgment as well as eliminating paying any taxes on the forgiven mortgage amount through the Mortgage Debt Relief Act via a short sale of their home. I'll discuss short sales in Chapter Seven, and how one may be a great option for you, too.

Chapter Three

Evaluating Your Situation

Study the past if you would divine the future.
—Confucius

Marjorie and Pete

Marjorie and Pete originally purchased their home in 1986 for $150,000, and raised their three children in the home. The children are now in their late teens and twenties with two in college and one a senior in high school.

Late in 2005, at a mandatory physical checkup dictated by the *changing of insurance carriers, Pete discovered he had cancer. It was operable, but the treatment course was aggressive. Though he made a full recovery, he missed a lot of work during chemo and radiation treatments. First sick days and then vacation time ran out quickly. Thankfully, despite his reduced hours, he and Marjorie still had health insurance, but the co–pays and deductibles amounted to thousands of dollars they just didn't have. They struggled to make payments on the debt. So, at the height of the real estate boom in 2005, they discovered that their home had doubled in value to $300,000. To help with out–of–pocket medical bills and tuition for their sons, they took out an equity loan on their home in the amount of $220,000.*

In 2007, Pete's 40 hours a week as a salesmen for an office–furniture distribution warehouse were cut back to 32 hours a week. Companies around the country were cutting back on "luxuries" such as new desks and chairs and conference tables and Pete saw his fellow employees laid off one by one. Frankly, he was just grateful to keep his job, even though his workload had increased.

In 2009, Marjorie stumbled on a curb and broke her ankle. She was on crutches and not mobile. With more and more medical bills looming, college for three kids, and Marjorie unable to work due to her accident and then treatment and recovery, and unable to keep up with their mortgage payments, they discovered that their home's price had fallen back to $150,000. They now owed more than the value of the home—they were underwater. They needed to get that mortgage payment down to a more manageable amount. This made Pete and Marjorie eligible for a loan modification, which they applied for and received, from their bank. Their payments are now more in line with their income and they are relieved to be able to keep their home.

***

If you're reading this, chances are that you have found yourself in a negative situation and you don't currently see a way out. Perhaps the future is looking a bit dim and scary. By picking up this book, you've reached out for help, and, often, asking for help is the hardest part. Congratulations on making that first step. I assure you, there is a light at the end of the tunnel and, even if it may feel like it, it's not an oncoming train.

The first step of changing your future is acknowledging your present. Before you determine where you want to go you must first determine exactly where you are today. In order to obtain a financial road map for the future you need both a destination as well as a starting point. That is what we will discuss in this first part of *The Homeowner Blueprint.*

Next, you need to figure out how you got to the point you are at now. Sometimes, the only way to see a path is to look behind us. This is as true in the financial arena as it is in nature. And while, it may not be pleasant, you need to get honest with yourself right now and figure out exactly how you got into the mess you currently find yourself in. Because sometimes, looking back is the only way to see your way forward.

If you're facing foreclosure and are behind on your payments, let me ask this: What happened? Was there a job loss? An illness? Both? No one, neither the bank nor the borrowers, agrees to enter into an agreement with the intention of losing the home to foreclosure. (If banks issued mortgage loans with the intentions of foreclosing, they wouldn't be banks for very long.)

Borrowers go into a mortgage wide–eyed with promises of a better tomorrow. But for those who end up in foreclosure, something along the way happens—perhaps more than one thing. For many people, the initial, obvious event is declining income. If both spouses were working when the mortgage loan was approved, the borrowers and the lender assume both will continue to work. If a husband and wife each make $5,000 per month and their monthly house payment is $2,500, the house payment is a respectable 25 percent of their gross monthly income of $10,000. This is called the *debt–to–income ratio*, and 25 percent is well below the typical maximum debt to income ratio of 33 percent that banks require to approve a mortgage.

Now, let's say, for the sake of example, that the husband is laid off from his job. He may be receiving unemployment, but it's not nearly enough to cover his old salary, as generally unemployment is only half of his actual previous earnings. It's a safety net, but not a strong or permanent one. If the husband, in this case, is unable to find a job, the unemployment payments typically run out after roughly 26 weeks, and when they do, this couple's 25 percent debt–to–income ratio now turns into 50 percent (Fig. 4).

Figure 4: Average Annual Unemployment Rate January 2003 to February 2013. Data compiled fromhttp://data.bls.gov/timeseries.LNS1400000, retrieved March 2013.

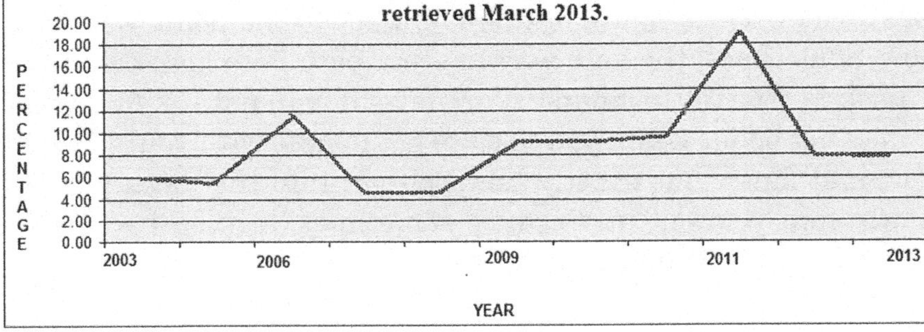

Let's change the scenario a bit. Maybe the husband wasn't laid off. Maybe his hours and pay were cut back, perhaps way back, like Pete's were. Let's say his salary was cut in half to $2,500 per month. Now the debt–to–income ratio is at 33 percent. This ratio is still within guidelines, but it is cutting it close, especially if there are other monthly obligations the couple must pay, such as car payments, college tuition, or braces for the kids. This isn't even taking into account any of life's little (or not–so–little) emergencies that don't show up as monthly payments—the car needs repairs, the water heater blows, the family dog gets sick, or worse, a family member gets sick. Small emergencies turn into financial catastrophes very quickly when a couple is living at a 33 percent debt–to–income ratio.

And what if our couple gets a divorce? When one party wants to keep the house, the judge will determine who keeps the property and who makes the mortgage payments. If the husband moves out of the house, he'll have to pay rent for his apartment and will also be responsible for making the mortgage payment of $2,500 per month on the old house.

Let's keep our couple married. However, what happens if the wife gets cancer? She's going to need treatment—office visits, lab tests, surgery, chemo, radiation, prescriptions. She's going to miss work. Her paycheck will be reduced or her employer may even be forced to replace her. Even if she has insurance, it might not cover everything. Now our couple has medical bills in addition to their regular monthly bills.

What if both spouses are perfectly healthy, both businesses they work for are unscathed by the downturn in the economy, but the wife's dad can no longer care for himself? Maybe they now shoulder the expense of care for him, be it in an extended care medical facility or just an assisted living center. Or the family moves him into the family home. Maybe they have to pay for in–home nursing care. Maybe the husband or wife has to quit their job to take care of him. That's a lot of maybes.

Lastly, there is one very unfortunate event that can propel someone into foreclosure. That sad reality is a death in the family. This can be the death of either the husband or the wife, or it could also be the result of a death of a family member such as a child or a parent. In addition to the devastating emotions experienced during a catastrophic loss of a spouse is the loss of income. Additionally, we each handle grief differently, and you or your partner may find yourself overcome and unable to work for a while which impacts your ability to make your monthly bills. You may need to go out of town to deal with a parent's estate. Every situation is different, but have no doubt; a death in the family can be devastating in more than one way.

You wouldn't want to wish any of these situations on anyone. Yet, they occur every day, thousands and thousands of times daily, all around the country. Sometimes bad things happen to good people, and there's just no way around it.

Evaluating Your Current Situation

In order to determine the best solution for you, you'll need to analyze your current financial situation and where it could be in the next 60 days. If you're behind and don't have a way to continue to make payments, then it's possible that 60 days is all the time you'll have until foreclosure is imminent. It's time to get real.

Balance Sheet

Review your own personal balance sheet. Essentially, a balance sheet is a list of assets and liabilities that will give you your net worth. If you don't have one, it's easy enough to draw one up with a pencil and pad. I've included a sample balance sheet in the back of the book which you can make copies of if you'd like to use it more than once. Right now, take a look at the balance sheet, and then come back. I've also got an example here for you to get an idea of how it looks. See Figure 5.

DEFINITIONS:

A balance sheet has three primary categories:

1. Liquid Assets— meaning cash or an asset easily converted to cash such as checking or savings accounts, bonds, money market instruments, trust funds, stocks, and some types of certificates of deposit—CDs. Liquid assets are anything you can convert to cash and carry with you.

2. Non–Liquid Assets— for example, real estate, notes, intellectual property, automobiles, collections, or any other sort of personal property that cannot be easily converted to cash. Non–liquid assets are anything that cannot be converted to cash quickly, or assets that must go through a lengthy process before conversion.

3. Liabilities—or debt. Liabilities are the payments you make to items that do not put cash in your pocket, i.e., credit cards, mortgage payments on a primary residence, mortgage payments on a rental property that is not covered by a tenant's rent, car and boat payments, timeshare payments, payments to installment debt such as furniture, televisions, laptops, and similar items.

Let's walk through an example of a balance sheet. This example is Pete and Marjorie's situation. As you can see, on the left–hand side you will itemize your current assets, both ***liquid*** and ***non–liquid.***

On the right–hand side; list your monthly obligations, or liabilities.

Assets		Liabilities	
Cash in Bank (Savings and Checking)	$3,000	Mortgage Loan Balance	$220,000
Stocks, Bonds, Mutual Funds	$2,000	Car Loan Balance	$ 5,250
Retirement Plans / 401(k)	$4,000	Credit Cards	$10,500
House Value	$150,000		
Automobile Value	$10,000	Total Liabilities	$235,750
Total Assets	$169,000	Net Worth (Assets – Liabilities)	- ($66,750)

Figure 5: Sample Balance Sheet

This table shows that a current net worth of –$66,750 (notice that number is negative) due to their home being upside down.

Now let's review the income and debt of this next example.

Income		Debt (Expenses)	
Marjorie's Salary	$0.00	Payments Monthly:	
monthUnable to work while recovering indefinitely		Car Payment	$229
on crutches		Mortgage Payment (PITIA*)	$1800
		- Mortgage	$1390
Pete's Salary	$5,000 / month	(principal and interest)	
Currently (80 percent – 32 hours/wk, former $6,250		- Taxes	$220
salary, now $5,000)		- Insurance	$125
		- Association Dues	$65
		Utilities (Gas, H2O, Lights)	$150
		Cable/Internet/Satellite	$36
		Cell Phones	$105
		Landline Phone	$15
		Credit Cards	$275
		Insurance (Life, Health, etc.)	$15
		Gas/Maintenance	$175
		Food	$200
Monthly Income:	$5,000	Monthly Liabilities:	$3,000 / month
		**PITIA: Principal, interest, taxes, insurance and association dues (if any).*	

Figure 6: Example Income and Debt.

We look at income and debt to establish a debt load, which is simply how much monthly debt is owed compared to the amount of monthly income. Underwriters call this your *Debt to Income Ratio*, or DTI. Monthly debt includes all payments required by lenders and credit agencies to maintain good credit worthiness. This list includes not just your mortgage and car payments, but utilities, personal cell phone and credit card payments, groceries, entertainment, gas, transportation, medical co–pays and prescriptions, insurance, private loan repayments, mortgage or car payments that you have co–signed on for family members, and any other monthly payment not included in this list that appears on your credit report or otherwise hinders you from making the mortgage payment in question. Money that is going towards other debt, in the view of a bank or lender, will not be going toward the mortgage.

Banks and underwriters use DTI ratios (debt to income) to factor in the unexpected. For this reason, if your debt load takes you past 33 percent, or whatever your lender's qualifying ratio is, when comparing your expenses to your gross income, then you will not qualify for this loan and you will need to look at another loan program or reduce the amount you are financing. If you look at it simply, if you are taxed 1/3 of your gross income, you receive 2/3 of your paycheck after taxes and other deductions. The bank is saying that 1/3 is a good qualifying ratio for many loan programs. If you receive 2/3 after taxes, they will let you buy a house as expensive as 1/3 of your paycheck and assume you can pay all your other expenses with the 1/3 you have left after taxes and your new mortgage payment to the bank. Does this sound like a very tight budget to anyone else? It does to me.

This should help you understand two things about DTI ratios. There are two ratios that a mortgage underwriter is looking at: First, your Housing Payment to Gross Income Ratio (HTI), and second, your Total Debt to Income Ratio (DTI). With a $1,800 total PITIA (Principal, Interest, Tax, Insurance and Association) payment, the HTI ratio for Pete and Marjorie would be ($1,800 ÷ $5,000 = 0.36 or 36 percent. The DTI would be $3,000 ÷ $5,000 = 0.60 or 60 percent, showing their total estimated debt load.

Current qualifying ratios for a mortgage modification under the Mortgage Debt Relief Act for a Home Affordable Modification Program (HAMP) modification requires a starting HTI greater than 31 percent. If this is the case, the underwriter can use tools like rate and balance reductions to bring the home loan payment to a more manageable number with respect to the new household income that is currently available to qualify to pay this mortgage after modification.

In this example, the debt load, or DTI, is 0.600 of Pete and Marjorie's gross monthly income ($3,000 ÷ $5,000) meaning their debt–

to–income ratio is 60 percent. If their take–home pay is $4,000 per month after deductions such as state and federal taxes, social security, health insurance premiums and so on, then that's what they have remaining to pay the mortgage and their car payment, and all other living expenses. As you can see in this example, there's not a whole lot left. Additionally, if they are taxed greater than the 20 percent I just assumed, and 1/3 of their gross income is withheld, then they are left with $3,333.33 in net cash to pay an estimated $3,000 in monthly liabilities.

Any large emergency like a pipe bursting in the house while away for the weekend, or a transmission failing while driving home from that weekend away, and there is not enough money in cash to cover large, unforeseen expenses, that becomes a problem. The options then are to leverage themselves greater with credit card debt or private loans, but when this is no longer possible, late payments start somewhere and the juggling act begins.

Improving the Balance Sheet

The first order of business is to increase the household income. Yet that's not really advice at all, that's a given. If finding a job or a new job, like Marjorie, for example, who is on crunches and cannot walk or drive, or getting a raise is not possible now, the other side of the coin is to reduce expenses. This is a relatively simple example. It's possible that your situation is likely crowded with more expenses than what is represented by the number listed here, yet the methodology is the same. For our couple above with one employed person in the house, Marjorie, for example, who is on crutches and cannot walk or drive, may have a difficult time finding employment after time out to recuperate.

First things first, to address the delinquent mortgage: Can you bring the loan balance of your mortgage current with the reserve funds you have? If you are two months behind on your mortgage with another monthly payment coming due, can you come up with, say, $5,400 in cash and still have enough money to keep the water running and lights on and still have money for food and other necessities?

If you are behind on two mortgage payments, and the next missed payment will trigger the foreclosure, can you at least make one payment? Even though you received the pre–foreclosure letter stating how much it will take to get current on your note, the bank won't begin foreclosure proceedings until you have missed three payments and they are each passed their grace period and delinquent. By making one payment and staying two payments behind, you'll be able to buy a little time, for now.

Next, let's look at the car payment. If your car payment is $229 per month, for example, that's $229 per month that could be going toward paying your mortgage instead. If the car loan balance is $5,250, it might make sense to pull some cash from one of your accounts and pay off the car loan entirely. On the other hand, maybe you can sell the car for $10,000, pay off the $5,250 car loan balance and put some cash in the bank. There are several reliable auto brands going for $4,000 or less, used, that you can buy until things get better. Remember, this exercise is about keeping you *out of foreclosure*, not keeping your dream car.

This example also shows that there is a retirement account balance of $4,000. Many retirement plans, whether a 401K, IRA or private pension, will allow for either a loan against that balance or what is called a "hardship" withdrawal to let you cash out your retirement funds without penalty. Check with your individual retirement plan and your financial advisor to confirm if there will be a penalty or not. A pre–foreclosure letter is certainly a hardship.

Homework: Prepare a balance sheet for your own finances.

Indicators of Imminent Default and Foreclosure

Now that you've laid out your current financial picture with a balance sheet and analyzed it, what do you see? If you see the chances of increased income in the very near future, that could be an indicator that all will be well soon. If finding another job or getting a raise is simply out of the picture, then foreclosure might be coming soon and you may already be in imminent default. If you find that you can't make up the past payments in time, and can't find additional sources of cash to pay off the past due balance, these are all indicators of an imminent default and foreclosure. If your situation sees absolutely no change with regard to assets, liabilities, or income, that's also a sign that often leads to foreclosure.

By identifying how you got where you are, and whether or not there are any apparent corrective measures that can be taken to move you away from foreclosure, then you'll need to proactively determine your next steps. We'll do that in the next chapter as we describe the foreclosure process in detail.

I'll explain how a loan modification works, like the one Marjorie and Pete received, in Chapter V.

Does this property look familiar? It should. It's the same property as seen in the photo at the beginning of this chapter, but some time after the housing market collapsed (p. 33).

Chapter Four

The Foreclosure Storm
All the Things That Happen

There are some things you learn best in calm, and some in storm.

—Willa Cather

A foreclosure can make even termites seem like a nice day at the park.

Olivia

Olivia is a single woman who got a good job in television production at the local cable news affiliate right out of college in 2007. She's made a name for herself as a sportscaster in the local arena. Olivia had worked her way through college watering plants for a stable of office complexes and graduated with no student loan debt. She has always lived within her means, no matter how meager they were. Within a year of starting her television job, she was able to buy a new home.

Unfortunately, like so many, she lost her job during the recession and has been unemployed for almost two years. She had unemployment insurance, which just barely kept her above water, but it has run out. She's just missed her second mortgage payment. The bank will be alerted to her financial situation and will be looking to talk to her about bringing her loan current before she misses a third payment and the foreclosure process starts.

Olivia is in luck, however. Due to an uncanny memory for numbers, Olivia's reputation has landed her a new job in another state as a college basketball statistician for a new all–sports network branching out into the area. She's not thrilled about moving, but after two years, she's pretty sure she's not going to find anything in her area. Not even watering plants in office buildings.

Her parents have offered to loan her the money to get caught up on her mortgage, and she'll make payments to them over the course of a year. In the meantime, she is going to rent her home out to a former colleague who still works at her station, and who can pick up the mortgage payments for her via rent payments.

Olivia has dodged the foreclosure bullet.

***

So, what exactly does someone experience throughout the foreclosure process? People who go through foreclosure rarely speak with their neighbors or friends regarding their personal financial problems, much less all the things that are happening to them, while the bank is in the process of taking back their home. What starts the entire foreclosure process?

It starts when you miss your first payment. That's right. You may not feel it immediately but lenders go on the alert when a single payment goes delinquent. Most mortgage documents are explicitly stated on the original note indicating that the mortgage payments are due on the first of each month and become past due on the 15th. Any payments made past the 15th are subject to a late payment penalty of approximately 5 percent of the outstanding monthly payment.

At this stage, however, even though the banks begin to put you on a watch list if you miss your first payment, they won't start getting nervous. When your payment is 20 days late, you can expect your phone to start ringing from the bank (these are typically robo–calls) reminding you to send in your payment either in person at a local bank branch, online, or by calling their customer service number where you can pay by credit, debit card, or check–by–phone.

When you miss the very next payment, or two in a row, three things occur: Your credit report will show that your mortgage payment is more than 30 days late, your credit score will begin to fall, and an official notice showing that you are 30 days late will be sent to you by certified mail from your lender. This is to remind you that your payment is due, and to document it in writing, just in case you continue to miss payments.

Notice of Default (NOD)

The NOD is a requirement. Mortgage lenders must formally notify borrowers via certified mail that a foreclosure is pending. It must further state that in order to avoid a foreclosure the borrower will need to immediately pay the two past–due payments in full. The borrower will be given an amount to pay, which will include two payments plus any late payment penalties. Some states require that the NOD be filed when three payments, not two, are missed. Generally, an NOD is sent when the loan is past due and delinquent. A NOD is sent when multiple payments are missed as a legal notification of delinquency. Active foreclosure is when a bank has sent all the required written notifications and legal forms and an NOD is attached to the front door of the property.

Understand it is more important for a payment to be delinquent than to be simply missed. A late payment is just that, late. A delinquent payment has passed 30 days late. If you have thirty days to make a payment and pay the late fee, you can scrape together the payment over that period.

For example: Your payment is due on October 1st and late after October 15th. On November 1st, you have another payment due and are now delinquent one payment. It has been approximately 30 days since October 1st at this point. Failure to pay through the end of November results in two payments due and on December 1st, your third payment is due since you last paid the mortgage. By the end of December you have three payments that are all passed 30 days late; in fact, you have October 1st's payment that is now 90 days delinquent, November 1st's payment that is 60 days delinquent and December 1st's payment that is now 30 days late. As you enter the new year with three payments more than 30 days late, you risk entering active foreclosure, having an NOD taped to your property's door for all to see, and it may be too late to pay one payment at a time to catch up. You may now have to reinstate the loan in full with all three payments, late fees and any fees incurred by the trustee assigned to reinstate your loan. It can go by before you know it.

The NOD must be filed as a public record at the county courthouse. Regardless of whether or not you want this information about your late payments being made public, it is readily available for those who want to look up this information at the courthouse. There are individuals and companies that scour this data on a daily or weekly basis.

Once the NOD is filed and made public, this is when you begin to receive solicitations in the mail via letters or postcards. These solicitations can come from attorneys, who've gotten your NOD records from the courthouse, and they want to represent you and help you file for bankruptcy, or individuals who want to "Pay Cash for Your House Today!" and companies with a variety of "help," including those who will talk to you about a loan modification...all for a fee, of course.

Your phone begins to ring even more frequently as the bank tries to contact you about your late payments, and at this point perhaps more than once a day. Usually it'll ring twice or more daily as you approach the end of the second month without any payment. If you ignore the phone calls, the calls will become more frequent. These calls are often made by computer and transferred to a live agent when contact is made.

When someone is in a financial crisis, the mortgage is typically not the only credit account that is having some problems. In fact, homeowners will typically let other credit accounts go bad before the mortgage becomes delinquent. If a homeowner has two or three credit cards outstanding, they'll often let the credit cards go into a collection account before they'll allow the mortgage to go into foreclosure.

Now, it's not just the mortgage company that is calling wanting their money; it's every other creditor you have that's calling as well. When people find themselves in such dire straits they often simply turn off the phone to keep it from ringing. As I counseled Olivia, I do not advise this. Ignoring the problem makes it worse, and the only assumption the creditor can make from silence is that things are getting worse not better. Each time a call is made, it is recorded in notes that an attempt to reach out to you was made. Lenders are required by law to call and work out something with you before foreclosure is possible. If they make a certain number of unanswered calls, their due diligence has been attempted and you will lose your home despite having never spoken with the bank. If they tried and you didn't, you lose. The one who follows the rules is the one that has the upper hand. It is extremely important that you know your local laws as each jurisdiction is different.

Repayment Plans

During this period, the bank really is trying to help you. They're not calling to scold you or to collect all the past due payments, though this would be ideal for both you and the bank to bring your loan current. Lenders have ***workout*** departments whose job it is to contact delinquent borrowers and set up a repayment plan to get caught up on the past–due mortgage and avoid foreclosure. Collection agents often have workouts that include taking delinquent payments and dividing them up over the next six or 12 months, adding the amount to the regular mortgage payment, allowing you to catch up over time while making slightly higher payments to pay back the difference.

For example, if you're three months behind on your mortgage and you speak to the workout department; they will review your financial statements regarding how much you currently make (income), and your current monthly expenses. By using these numbers they can determine whether or not you have enough income to satisfy the mortgage in the future.

Often, borrowers get behind for a couple of months and don't have the funds to send three or four months' worth of housing payments to the bank, yet a workout department can divide that delinquency into monthly payments that can be spread out over three, six, or even 12 months. The important thing to understand here is that you will need to be OUT of your hardship for this to be extended to you. That is, you will need to demonstrate that the hardship is behind you. You cannot be in a continuous hardship and move forward paying MORE each month to catch up if you are STILL in your financial hardship. It is simple to understand when you speak with the agent offering you the workout.

For example: If you stopped making your mortgage payment because your spouse lost their job, for whatever reason, and they continue to be unemployed with no income, then you are still in your hardship situation and payments, plus the portion you now have to pay back, will be almost impossible since you struggle to pay the payment by itself. Now, if your spouse lost their job causing the hardship, but now they are 100 percent re–employed with equal or greater salary, your hardship is behind you and larger payments while paying back the delinquent payments may be possible.

Olivia talked to her bank's workout department, told them her situation, and of her new job starting in another state the following month. With her acquisition of a new job, at slightly more than her previous job's pay, Olivia was eligible for a repayment plan. She told them she wanted to talk to her parents and would call back in a couple of days. The bank said they would wait 48 hours. The bank will always verify your new employment and may require a month's worth of paystubs from the new position to verify the income. There is no trust in banking, only what you can prove.

Foreclosure

If this is your situation, and you are greater than three payments behind, and you can afford a repayment plan with a workout, this is your best choice at this stage. It allows you to bring the loan current without any creative solutions. You simply pay the money back over the next few months or a year and move forward. If you can't afford any payment, you'll go into another, more advanced stage of the foreclosure process.

When the next payment is missed, the lender will then notify you that you are now in active foreclosure and they will proceed to recover the house from you, legally, and evict you. Active foreclosure simply means that your loan has been labeled "In Foreclosure" on the bank's internal systems. I have seen loans up to 12 or 24 payments delinquent that are not in "active foreclosure" due to either efforts of the homeowner to work things out with the bank, or the bank has simply not done the due diligence required by the state to proceed with foreclosure.

As a side note, and I touched on this in Chapter I: an issue banks are having is that they have to reproduce the original documents required for the foreclosure process, and many banks simply cannot do so. The process of securitizing loans in bundles to sell as traded assets required the destruction of many promissory notes, since an asset traded on Wall Street cannot carry a promissory note to another person or owner while it is traded. There is no way to know how many loans were treated this way, and some homeowners do not understand why they continue to live in a home without paying the mortgage and are not receiving more notifications regarding foreclosure, workout processes or any options at all. See Chapter I for more.

You will receive another certified letter informing you of the imminent foreclosure. The lender will provide you with a ***Redemption or Reinstatement Quote*** that you can pay to stop the foreclosure process entirely. Stopping the foreclosure by paying this amount is called your ***Right of Redemption***.

The lender will then allow you to pay off the past due balance and provide you with an amount it would take to keep the home and the mortgage. The redemption amount will include all the past due mortgage payments, your next mortgage payment, plus all accrued legal fees incurred by the bank's attorneys.

If you are unable to gather and pay the redemption amount directly to the trustee (at this point you cannot bring the loan current directly with the bank, and you must pay the trustee who pays the bank to bring the loan current), the foreclosure process will continue. At this point in the foreclosure process, the lender will set the date at which the property will be sold at auction. Generally, depending on local regulations, two weeks before the sale date, the official notice of the date of sale will be publicly posted and recorded with the trustee in charge of the actual sale auction on the bank's behalf—based on their local requirements and guidelines. It could be a posting in the courthouse, a small ad in a newspaper or legal publication, or now, many cities post sale dates online.

Five days before the sale, you, the borrower, have lost all possibilities of re–instating the loan. On the date of sale, all interested parties will gather at the courthouse steps, or appropriate location, and wait for the lender to give a starting bid or reserve bid amount. In some cases, the lender purchases the property at auction by paying the minimum bid as well as the outstanding mortgage because the reserve is not met. In other cases, large hedge funds, corporations and real estate investors compete against each other for the right to purchase the property. The winner, of course, is the one with the most cash or largest cashiers check. The ownership of the property is awarded immediately after declaring the buyer and total cash funds are presented to the trusteThis process is called a non–judicial foreclosure, meaning it did not go to court in front of a judge.

A judicial foreclosure process works in a similar manner but has a few differences. A judicial foreclosure means the lender's original note did not grant "power of sale" authority to the lender. A power of sale clause allows the lender to foreclose on the property without going in front of a judge. Absent the power of sale clause, the lender must go in front of a judge, prove that the mortgage foreclosure process has been legal, and the judge will award the lender the home and the mortgage.

Another key difference between a judicial and non–judicial foreclosure process involves deficiency judgments. A lender may not seek to obtain a deficiency judgment when a home is foreclosed upon by way of non–judicial foreclosure. The percentage of judicial versus non–judicial states is about even. A quick Internet search can tell you which type is used in the state where you live and the process you have to go through to reinstate your loan. Contacting the trustee directly will also help. Their information is on the Notice of Default and can be found by calling your bank. The trustee's name is attached to your file as soon as there is a need to do so.

Deficiency Judgments

Deficiency judgments can occur on all sorts of cases where personal property is secured by a note. But what, you might ask, is a deficiency judgment?

Put simply, a deficiency judgment is a court ruling that makes you liable for the difference between what the bank can get for selling your debt and the debt that is actually owed.

For example, someone buys a car, finances it, and the bank takes it back due to non–payment. Say there is a $10,000 outstanding car note balance that the borrower couldn't pay. After the bank takes back the car, it will sell the car for whatever it can get, either to the general public or on a wholesale basis by selling to an automobile dealer or automobile auction house. If the bank sells the car for $6,000, there is still $4,000 unaccounted for remaining on the loan. The bank can file a lawsuit to recover the $4,000 deficiency and obtain a judgment. If the bank wins the judgment, this will appear on the consumer's credit report for seven years, either as a "paid" judgment or as an "unpaid" judgment, depending on whether or not—as implied by the description—you pay the amount the judge dictates.

Banks can also sue homeowners who do not have protection against deficiency judgments for payment. Some mortgages have this protection built into their original contracts. In most cases, this protection is issued to the homestead (primary residence) for mortgages used to purchase real estate. This protection, however, may disappear when a homeowner refinances out of the original–purchase mortgage, eliminating the deficiency protection.

For example, the bank could sell a property for $100,000 where the outstanding mortgage balance was $200,000. The bank could then file, when allowed, a deficiency suit against the foreclosed homeowner for the difference, in this case, for $100,000. Without assets to pay this difference, the debt looms until it is resolved through bankruptcy, cash payment or other negotiation with the lender. In most cases, banks with will foreclose on other assets like cars, boats, or property until they are paid in full or satisfied.

In Nevada, a bank has three months after the sale date in order to file for a deficiency judgment. In California, state law allows both judicial and non–judicial foreclosure processes, but deficiency judgments are only awarded when foreclosed via a judicial foreclosure. You can check online to determine if you live in a judicial or non–judicial state; realtytrac.com is a reliable source to check your state.

If you miss one payment, but are able to make it up, then none of this will happen to you. If you miss two payments, the foreclosure wheels will really start to spin. This is the situation that Olivia once found herself. This is not something that will go away. Without a game plan, you could be without your home, no mortgage, and foreclosed upon. You need to review your options and review them well. We'll discuss those options in the next chapter.

Olivia is lucky that her parents are able and willing to loan her the cost of 60 days, plus fees and other charges, for her late mortgage payment and get her completely out of foreclosure. Once she begins earning that steady paycheck, she can pay them back, with interest.

Chapter Five

Bankruptcy

Abraham Lincoln, P.T. Barnum, Walt Disney, John James Audubon, Mickey Rooney, Buffalo Bill, Gary Burghoff, Mark Twain, John Connally, Francis Ford Coppola, Donald Trump.

What do all these people have in common? They all filed for bankruptcy protection either as an individual or a corporation.

Vicki and Richard

Vicki and Richard are brother and sister. They inherited the family home from their late parents. Rather than selling, they decided to live in the house. They'd been roommates during their college years earlier and they'd gotten along well, so it sounded like a fun way to revisit those good old days while also saving money.

As the house was paid in full and loans were easy to get, they took out a large equity mortgage—about 80 percent of the home's value at that time—to make renovations and improvements to the home. They figured as long as they were taking out a loan that would surely be easy to pay off with the home's equity over time (after all, property always goes up in value, right?) they both bought new cars, and they took a luxury vacation to the Caribbean.

Their timing was less than ideal. The equity mortgage was higher than the value of the home within the first year.

Before they even had time to entertain their friends with all their great stories of the Caribbean, both became victims of the recession. Vicki found she was a little more expendable than she thought at her job in the college admissions department and Richard learned people didn't need housing development planners when they stopped building housing developments. Unemployed, narrowly employable to begin with, unemployment ticking away, it didn't take long to fall behind on those monster mortgage payments.

They applied for a HAMP I restructuring, but with no jobs or other incoming cash options on the horizon, they were not eligible. They were unsure whether they should do a Chapter 7 or 13 bankruptcy, a deed in lieu, a short sale, or just walk away. They were devastated by the idea of losing the family home but, at this point, without an influx of cash, their options were limited.

They were also looking at having nowhere to live if they lost the home.

***

Along with other offers to "help" you as you navigate your real estate storm, there may be the offer from attorneys to help manage, reduce, or eliminate your current debt load by way of filing for bankruptcy.

There are two basic types of bankruptcy petitions that an individual or couple may file. Bankruptcy laws are drawn from federal statute and do not vary from state to state and offer two variations of debt adjustments, or bankruptcy: Chapter 7 and Chapter 13 filings.

There are some types of debt, however, that may not be eliminated or reduced by a bankruptcy filing: income taxes, sales tax, student loans, child support, alimony, and mortgages. That's right: filing for bankruptcy will not free you up from past–due mortgage payments. You will still have to make up those delinquent payments. Richard and his sister, Vicki, quickly found this out.

The benefit of a bankruptcy is not to eliminate past–due mortgage payments but to *eliminate other consumer debt*. This may free up your income to help make your mortgage payments or the past–due payments to be spread out over as long as a five–year period. Look at both types of filings to see how they can affect an impending foreclosure.

Chapter 13 Bankruptcy

A Chapter 13 bankruptcy is sometimes called a "wage earners" plan. This filing does not eliminate any past–due debt but establishes a repayment plan that the consumer must adhere to. If the consumer does not follow the repayment plan and begins to miss the rescheduled payments, the court could declare the bankruptcy as void and the total amount due will be required, just as it was prior to the filing.

If you file for a Chapter 13, the court will ask you to provide additional documentation when you present your bankruptcy plea. This paperwork will include:

- Bankruptcy petition
- List of all creditors outstanding, the balance owed each creditor, and current monthly payments
- Copies of the previous six months bank and investment statements
- Most recent paystubs from your employer
- W–2s and 1099s from the previous two years
- Signed and dated tax returns from the previous two years
- Evidence of completing a consumer credit counseling course
- A repayment plan on how you propose to repay your obligations

Once you submit the forms, the court will then assign a trustee, who will oversee both the implementation of the agreed upon repayment period and amounts being paid, in a timely manner. In addition, once you file for bankruptcy, all efforts by creditors to get money from you must immediately stop.

Your outstanding debts will be totaled and compared with your disposable income. Disposable income is income you can use for consumption or saving. This is the income you have left over after all expenses, utilities, payments, taxes, deductions, and other debt or credit requiring payment. Some people spend all of their money before they have it in hand on consumption and do not save. Others pay all of their monthly payments and only spend a portion of what is left; that they understand is their disposable income, after savings.

The trustee will determine the proper amount that should be paid back each month while still allowing you to keep your automobile, your home, and other secured debt you wish to keep. You will make your monthly payments to the trustee who will then disburse them to the outstanding creditors. You can see how important it is to work with a reputable bankruptcy firm or attorney, as they are the go–between from you to clearing your name and payment record with your lenders. Repayment periods can be as short as 36 months or as long as 60 months. Once the repayment plan has been completed, the Chapter 13 bankruptcy will then be filed as "discharged" and your financial life begins anew.

Chapter 7 Bankruptcy

A Chapter 7 bankruptcy is a complete discharge of all debt, not including the non–dischargeable debts of mortgage, student loans, alimony, child support, and income taxes.

While a Chapter 7 will not temporarily alleviate past–due mortgage payments nor stop a foreclosure, the benefit of a Chapter 7 bankruptcy is the ability to free up monthly income previously used to pay other debts and instead devote that income to the mortgage payments.

The paperwork required for the Chapter 7 is much the same as it is for a Chapter 13 filing.

- Bankruptcy petition;
- List of all creditors outstanding, the balance, and current monthly payments;
- Copies of the previous six months bank and investment statements;
- Most recent paystubs from your employer;
- W–2s and 1099s from the previous two years;
- Signed and dated tax returns from the previous two years;
- Evidence of completing a consumer credit counseling course.

Any secured property you wish to keep may be excluded from the bankruptcy. You would reaffirm the debt, sign new documents, make the payments and keep the secured property. If you have secured property you do not wish to keep (like a second car), it would be included in the bankruptcy filing.

For example, if you owe $20,000 on an auto loan and include that auto loan in the bankruptcy you do not get to keep the vehicle. However, you will not have to pay the auto loan any longer. The company that financed your auto loan will come to your home and pick up the vehicle, and it can't try to get the money from you at any point down the road. The aforementioned deficiency judgments are waived or simply not granted in this process, so your debt is essentially forgiven.

There are exemptions in a bankruptcy. Exemptions are those assets that the trustee may allow you to keep such as an automobile that you use to drive to work. There are limits to an automobile exemption, and allowances can be made for you to keep the automobile if the value of the automobile is below state limits. However, if you own two cars, and one of them is a late model BMW, be prepared to have that vehicle impounded and sold in order to pay off creditors.

Exemptions from a bankruptcy filing are typically listed by dollar amount associated with the asset. For example, California has multiple exemptions including a limit for a motor vehicle at $3,525 and an exemption amount for personal jewelry and works of art of $7,175. Nevada also has a complete list of exempted items and associated limits for things such as household goods, jewelry, and other items. For a complete list of exempted items and their associated limits in dollar amounts, consult your attorney or visit the appropriate state's bankruptcy exemption list. Another good place for information is the United States Department of Justice website: http://www.justice.gov/ust/eo/ust_org/bky-info/index.htm.

A Chapter 7 covers all outstanding debt, collection accounts, and judgments. It essentially wipes the slate clean and doesn't set up repayment plans for your creditors, but it does not give you time to repay your overdue mortgage payments. Your bank will still proceed with a foreclosure.

While Chapter 7 might seem the easier of the two, there is a "means test," which limits individuals who may and may not file for a complete discharge of debts using a Chapter 7 bankruptcy. This means test averages all your income over the previous six months and uses that amount as your qualifying income. Your qualifying income must be less than the median income for a household in the state in which you live. If your income is below the median income, you can file the Chapter 7. If it is above, you have no choice but to file for Chapter 13.

Bankruptcies and Credit

A bankruptcy will appear twice on a credit report: once, when it is first filed, and again on the date it was discharged. A Chapter 7 bankruptcy petition can take just a couple of weeks if there are few creditors. A Chapter 13 bankruptcy petition will take quite a bit longer due to the additional amount of information that needs to be reviewed, approved and then implemented by the trustee.

A Chapter 7 bankruptcy will remain on your credit report for 10 years. A Chapter 13 will stay on your credit report for seven years from the initial filing date as long as the repayment plan was completed within the parameters of the agreed upon terms. If the Chapter 13 was not completed due to non–repayment, that information will stay on the report for 10 years as well.

While that seems scary, in reality, you're not doomed for a decade when you file for bankruptcy. In fact, you will soon see credit offers from credit card companies. These companies issue credit cards to those fresh out of bankruptcy or who are experiencing negative credit. However, if you do obtain credit after a bankruptcy and falter on it as well, it's quite possible that a mortgage lender will deny you another mortgage while the credit reflects a bankruptcy. It's very important to *never, ever* be late on any other credit item after a bankruptcy discharge if you want to be considered for a mortgage loan in the future. Be very judicious when accepting and using any new offers of credit. You don't want to end up right back where you started again.

Your credit scores will remain low for the next few years. Even the slightest 30–day late payment on a department store credit card can harm your future chances of obtaining a home mortgage.

Vicki and Richard had limited options. What they ended up doing was to sell both new cars—a Lexus and a Humvee—and they were able to compile enough cash to hold off the bank for several more months. In the meantime, they needed to quickly research their options before making a final decision. After careful consideration and discussion with me, they opted for a Chapter 13 restructuring in Richard's name only—a brother and sister cannot file a joint Chapter 13. They feel confident that in the time given by the court, the federal extension of unemployment benefits, and the fact that they are both taking night classes to gain new skills to broaden their job opportunities, they feel that they are on the right path to save the family home.

Chapter Six

Loan Modifications and Deed in Lieu: Bank Profit Centers

"...so do I answer you:
The pound of flesh, which I demand of him,
Is dearly bought; 'tis mine and I will have it.
If you deny me, fie upon your law!

—William Shakespeare, *The Merchant of Venice*

Robert and Gayle

Robert and Gayle bought their home in Southern California shortly before their 2004 wedding. They have lived in the home since that time. After the birth of their first child, Gayle quit her job to stay at home with the baby and then stayed home to mother the subsequent children. She enjoyed being at home with her children, and never regretted giving up her career, even though she knew at the time that the gap in her employment history would make it difficult for her to ever go back.

Robert and Gayle were planners. From the moment they married, they put away money for a rainy day. They never spent extravagantly, instead taking any extra money they had and putting it away for the future. Robert, who worked as an engineer for his local city government, turned down offer after offer from private companies, always choosing the stability of a government job over the vagaries of the private sector.

In 2010, after the third round of layoffs in Robert's department due to city budget cuts, Robert lost his job. The family survived on unemployment insurance and their savings.

In the fall of 2012, Robert found a permanent position with an up–and–coming private company that paid well. He and Gayle applied for a loan modification; however, their mortgage and home remained in continuing foreclosure proceedings despite their application. The clock was ticking.

Luckily for Robert and Gayle and many other Californians caught in this waiting game, the law was changed. As of January 1, 2013, foreclosure proceedings continuing while the homeowner applied for a loan modification, also known as "dual tracking," was eliminated under the ***California Homeowner Bill of Rights*** *(http://oag.ca.gov/hbor).*

Gayle and Robert were able to stop the foreclosure proceedings because of the new rules, and they got the time they needed for their loan modification based on Robert's new income. They then had the time for the modification to be approved, and then to catch up on their missed payments, and save their home. With Robert finding a new job, they had the money to catch up, but it took the changing of the California law to give them the time they needed.

***

In each single year between 2008 and 2012, as many as 3.5 million homes have been foreclosed upon in the United States. California leads the number of foreclosures by a wide margin with a combination of both a soft economy (many wage earners do not make what they used to), and the sheer number of homes (much of the sub–prime mortgage lending was concentrated in California). The combination of a larger percentage of sub–prime loans than the national average, plus the fact that they have more homes than most states, leads to California having the *most* foreclosures in number.

While foreclosure trends are leveling off, they have not subsided, they are continuing. In order for foreclosures to taper off, the overall economy will need to improve. Many homeowners are having a rough go of it primarily due to job loss and problems finding new work. Unemployment rates in the United States have risen above the 8 percent mark as of February 2009, and surpassed the 10 percent level in October 2009. Since then, the unemployment rate has remained above 8 percent as of September 2012 (United States Department of Labor, 2013). This is an unprecedented mark and rivals the unemployment the country experienced in the Great Depression years (1929 – 1939), see Figure 4, p. 36.

The country has been divided in a constant debate about how to create jobs and get the economy moving. Different government programs are being initiated in an attempt to thwart the foreclosure wave and keep people in their homes. While some of these programs, including the Home Affordable Refinance Program (HARP) of 2009 and the allegedly new and improved HARP II of 2012, were drawn up to save homeowners from foreclosure, they did little to stop the process. Some homeowners were successful using these programs, although most banks complain that the government guidelines are too confusing and require too much work. Many banks either decline HARP applications or refuse to accept applications altogether (Tracy and Wright, 2012).

A traditional refinance program prior to HARP required that the loan amount be, at most, 90 percent of the value of the home. This didn't help those whose homes were underwater. HARP I allowed for homeowners to refinance their properties under new, lower interest rates set by the government and provided higher loan limits. HARP II further relaxed loan limit guidelines. Homeowners wishing to take advantage of the HARP program still have to prove the ability to repay the new refinanced loan. This means, qualify with acceptable HTI and DTI ratios as we discussed earlier. Many cannot, as their incomes have fallen due to the economy and continuing furloughs and/or layoffs. If the homeowner can qualify for the program, it is still difficult to find a bank that will work with a HARP applicant.

Seeing that these programs were making little headway, the government issued yet another program, the Home Affordable Modification Program, or HAMP. HAMP was also initially introduced in 2009, and an updated program was released in June of 2012. The HAMP program allowed for the changing of the loan terms of the original note by way of an in–house mortgage refinance. HAMP's primary function is to drop the interest rate down so that the homeowner will meet the current debt–to–income ratio of under 31 percent currently. Again, expect this number to adjust up or down at any given time due to government regulation or update.

This program has also seen limited success primarily due to the economic conditions of the borrowers. If someone is having problems making a $2,000 per month mortgage payment, they might also have problems making a $1,500 per month payment. In so many situations, it is less an interest rate problem as much as it is a lack of income problem. This is apparent in the default rates of loans that have been refinanced under these programs. Many loans have been modified only to return to the delinquent side of the bank. This is further evidence that interest rates are not at fault; rather income cannot support such a big loan. Simply put, oftentimes before the crisis, people bought homes that they could not afford and modifying the rate down cannot mitigate the fact that a buyer has financed more than their income could afford.

Depending on the type of program, HARP, HARP II, HAMP, or HAMP II, nearly half of all homeowners who participated in these government programs became delinquent yet again within 12 months. This can lead to the conclusion that while these programs may provide temporary relief, they may not be a long–term solution to avoid foreclosure. The bottom line is people need homes they can afford, not slight modifications to loans they cannot.

Loan Modification

The introduction of new government programs was both a response to the rapid rise of foreclosures, and also the growth of a new industry—loan modifications.

Loan modifications have been a part of a bank's big bag of tricks since the introduction of mortgages. Historically, if interest rates dropped, a borrower could contact their bank and ask for a modification of their loan instead of a refinance. When banks retained ownership of their loans and used their own money to finance them, they were in more control of any future repayment and negotiation of changes.

A modification amends the loans original terms. If a bank holds the loan paper, they can change the terms as they see fit since it is their loan and their money. There are only four terms that make up a mortgage loan: **The Principal Balance, the Term (or time in months or years), the Interest Rate and the Payment**. If we are trying to adjust the payment, we must change one of the other three terms. In the beginning of the government assistance programs, interest rate and term changes were made to lower the payment, but the mortgage principal balance was not addressed. This left many homeowners with a house that had an "affordable" payment compared to their income, but a house that was still leveraged well passed its current value. Today, underwater mortgages can be written down to nearly 110 percent of today's market value. One of the reasons so many government–funded modifications failed in the first twelve months is due to the fact that homeowners were realizing that they were still paying to live in a home that was not worth the loan they were paying on it. Some people legitimately experienced further hardship, but some homeowners simply do not want to give money to live in a house that has a loan far larger than its value.

A modification simply changes parts of the original note, in the simplest case, the interest rate is lowered and the lender keeps the mortgage. A refinance pays off the old mortgage completely, typically with a brand new lender.

As banks found their mortgage holdings becoming more and more delinquent and foreclosure rates on the rise, they began to solicit their borrowers offering them loan modifications. This is the situation Robert and Gayle fortunately found themselves. A loan modification works similarly to a refinance or any other mortgage application yet with much less paperwork. A loan modification will typically require:

- Most recent bank and investment statements;
- Most recent paycheck stubs;
- A hardship letter;
- A signed modification application;
- Tax Returns (most recent 2 years);
- 4506T (Authorization to release tax info).

When a homeowner applies for a loan modification, the lender evaluates:

- The current income situation;
- Assets;
- Credit report.

The lender can then determine the new interest rate, dropping it low enough to meet standard debt ratio guidelines.

The lender will determine affordability by comparing current debt and the new mortgage payment with current, verified income. Many lenders won't modify a mortgage unless the mortgage is behind on payments and some only if more than 90 days late. However, being delinquent on your mortgage is not a requirement for modification under the HAMP program. These government plans are hardship programs and late payments help document hardship, but being behind on your mortgage is not explicitly required for government loan assisted modification. It is required 100 percent of the time to document financial hardship and some bank agents will tell you that you must be behind to qualify. In some cases modifications on the bank's side show unavailable due to "loan has not lost good standing." If you are caught in this cycle and do not want to go delinquent, keep calling agents and seek additional help. Think about it though, if you always find the money to stay current, the bank's normal "triggers" do not alert them to an imminent default situation, as if the loan were indeed behind in payment. If the loan modification is approved—whether through a government program or a private lender—the homeowner makes the new mortgage payments based upon the new, lower amount.

Keep in mind that just because the mortgage is 90 days late doesn't mean the bank necessarily has started the foreclosure process. The lender has the ability to start the process at 90 days past due, but in some cases chooses to wait until a later date. This does not keep the homeowner from adjusting the loan or loan terms with the bank. In most cases, the foreclosure processes starting actually motivates the bank and the homeowner to re–examine the mortgage terms.

Loan modifications can make a lot of sense if everything falls into place. But there are some things you need to be aware of when considering a loan modification.

First, you will need to determine if your financial situation will improve or stabilize in order to continue making timely payments. If you default on your loan modification, you won't get another chance with that lender and the foreclosure wave will start yet again. In Robert's case, he was able to find a new job giving his family the income they needed to bring their finances and lifestyle back up to a pre–unemployment level.

Second, you need to make sure you don't extend the length of your mortgage yet again when you get the loan modification. Say you bought your house four years ago on a 30–year mortgage with a 6.00 percent interest rate on a $300,000 mortgage. Your monthly mortgage payment is $1,798. You have now made payments for four years. Your loan modification may be at a lower interest rate with a lower payment, but for an additional 30 years. The modification program can push the term out to a maximum of 40 years if the drop in interest rate does not bring the loan back to affordability, the clock has started all over again, and sometimes the clock has added more time than the original mortgage indicated.

You can check online to determine your amortization schedule: http://www.bankrate.com/calculators/mortgages/mortgage-calculator.aspx?MSA=6720&MSA=6720

Let's break down this amortization schedule and see what just happened.

Of that first mortgage payment, $1,500 of that is interest that goes directly to the bank. In the first year, you made total payments of $21,583, with $17,899 of that going toward interest and the remaining $3,684 going to the principal and therefore paying down the mortgage.

That's how mortgage loans are calculated, with the bulk of the interest payments made near the beginning of the loan term and little going toward the principal. The original principal balance is not paid down much until year 19 on a 30–year mortgage when the amounts going to principal finally exceed the amount that goes to interest.

If you modify your mortgage and get a lower rate and your loan term is extended for another 30 years, your bank will have the advantage of resetting the mortgage. All of the money that you have paid until that time has no affect on the balance of the principal.

Banks don't mind a loan modification as long as they think they'll get their money back. In return for making a bet that the homeowner will pay them back on time, a significant amount of interest will accrue for the lender. Do you see the benefit to them?

Banks can appreciate the power of a loan modification as it can increase the possibility of increased interest earnings instead of losing that interest by way of a foreclosure. You get to keep the house and avoid foreclosure and the bank continues to receive payments from you in the form of additional interest they would not have otherwise received.

Also, it's important to remember that nearly half of such modifications fail to perform over the 12 months following the modification. If your modification fails to bring you to affordability, you'll be facing foreclosure yet again, where you struggle to make the payments, again, all while losing still more money to the bank. A loan modification is successful if you can be assured that your current financial situation has already improved or will improve over the next year, like Robert did by way of a new job, or additional income or an unexpected financial windfall such as an inheritance or gambling winnings.

Deed-in-Lieu

A *deed-in-lieu* is a shortened term for "deed in lieu of a foreclosure." Perhaps the simplest method to avoid foreclosure, this is when the homeowner agrees to sign over all rights to the property by way of signing over the deed to the bank. This is a deed transfer ***instead of*** a foreclosure but it will affect your credit in nearly the same way. Although this is an option in some cases, it's not one I would regularly recommend. It makes getting a deficiency judgment waiver difficult and without knowing the market value of the house, you may be giving equity to the bank instead of traditionally selling the home to pay off the loan.

In order for you to get a deed–in–lieu, your bank will need to agree with this procedure, it's not something you can initiate and approve on your own terms. Additionally, the bank will need to perform a thorough title search, making sure there are no other liens or judgments on your property. Say, for instance, there is a second mortgage on your home. While the holder of the first mortgage might accept a deed–in–lieu, the holder of the second mortgage may not, cancelling any deed in lieu request. Lastly, any judgments or property tax liens must be cleared prior to any deed transfer.

If a foreclosure is imminent and you feel you're in a situation where you would rather walk away from the property and hand it back to the lender, your bank will likely appreciate a deed–in–lieu if they're convinced a foreclosure is their only other answer. In order to foreclose on a property, banks have to spend time and money on attorneys, staff, and associated foreclosure costs that can run into the thousands. With a deed–in–lieu, a bank avoids significant foreclosure expenses. Unfortunately, you will still lose your house using this method. However, because of the negative credit effect, most homeowners avoid this option. That would be my recommendation in most cases.

Chapter Seven

Short Sale
The Best Underwater Mortgage Option?

Do not speak of life
as if a freshly pressed suit—
It is only through our wrinkles,
rips and stains
we know we've lived
at all.

—Charles O'Hay, Poet

Stephanie

Stephanie is a widowed mom of two boys. Her sons are both in middle school. After her husband's death in an auto accident, she received $100,000 in life insurance, and she used a large part of that to buy the home she and her boys have lived in since 2001. She had a good, stable job doing ad design in a marketing firm since the late 1990s. Unfortunately her firm downsized in 2009, and she was laid off. She has been unable to find permanent work since.

Stephanie manages to make her mortgage payment every month through a combination of government programs like Supplemental Nutritional Assistance Program (SNAP), Unemployment Insurance, and a few part–time jobs here and there in addition to her virtual craft shop online at Etsy.com, an eBay company, where she sells crocheted item. There is barely enough at the end of the month to cover other expenses like heating, electricity, and school supplies. Her house is now severely underwater and the debt is weighing heavy on her every month. The home's value has fallen to nearly 50 percent less than its original pre–bubble value when she bought it in 2001.

Stephanie lives in constant fear that something will go wrong—the car will break down, one of her kids will get sick, the part–time work won't come through—and her whole world will fall apart. She feels the precariousness is killing her. Her kids feel the stress too.

Stephanie has met with Legal Aid about the possibility of just walking away from the home. After all, she will never be able to pay off the loan in her lifetime. Unfortunately, if she walks away, the bank could come after her for the difference between what they sell the house for and what her original mortgage balance was when she went into foreclosure (a deficiency judgment).

After careful consideration, and my advice, she's decided to go through a short sale, which will give her the opportunity to buy a new property, with more manageable payments, in a few years. She's feeling much better about the future.

***

So far you've read about the various options open to you that can help navigate and understand your foreclosure and/or underwater mortgage real estate storm. First, it's important to realize that you do have options and you're not alone in this situation.

We've gone through several of the options available so far for both foreclosure and underwater mortgages. In my opinion, the best option for the *underwater* homeowner is a short sale. But before going into detail about how that works, first we need to understand exactly what is...and what is not...a short sale.

What is, and why is it called, a "short sale"? It is called a short sale because the bank that holds your mortgage has agreed to accept less than what is owed on the mortgage loan as payment in full without any recourse. A "no recourse" loan means a loan where the bank may not attempt to collect other assets from you in order to satisfy a mortgage loan balance. A short sale means the bank accepts your offer to pay off the balance and there is no further collection activity by the bank in the form of a deficiency judgment waiver.

Let's look at an example: Stephanie's current mortgage balance when we first met was $250,000 and she knew that similar homes in her area were selling for $150,000, which is less than half of what they were selling for just a few short years ago.

In this scenario, she is underwater by ($250,000 – $150,000 =) $100,000. If she sold the property to avoid foreclosure or bankruptcy, she would have to bring an additional $100,000 to the closing table, along with closing costs associated with selling a home, including real estate commissions, title, escrow and associated charges. Money that she does not have or else she would not be in this situation.

With a short sale, she'll forego bringing the $100,000 shortfall to the closing table. The bank agrees to accept a lower amount to settle the outstanding mortgage loan that the bank will then list as being paid in full. In this example, a bank would accept the new buyer's offer of $150,000. The final sales price can be whatever amount you, or Stephanie in this case, the buyer, and the bank agree upon mutually.

A short sale works like most any other sale when it comes to the selling process. You will list your property for sale, find a buyer, and close on the home. You avoid foreclosure and bankruptcy and can move on to home ownership again, and much sooner than either of those processes on your record would allow.

But before you get to the selling process, you must have the bank agree to the short sale amount in advance. The bank will ask you to document your situation before the bank can approve the short sale. The bank is not going to allow you to short sale your house because you no longer want it and it is not worth what it once was. You are both in this situation together having once agreed on a price and terms of a loan. You will need to document how your life has changed, how it has created a financial hardship, and how you can no longer make payments on this loan. With that documented, you stand a much better chance to short sale the property.

The first thing to do is, like Stephanie, to contact your bank and tell their representative that you would like to prepare a short sale offer. They will give you a list of documents you will need to provide them. This is called the "short sale package." The initial steps require you to list the property for short sale with a Realtor® and supply the bank with an *Authorization to Release Financial/Loan Information* document authorizing your Realtor® to work on your loan and short sale.

The first document the bank will review once your file is actively listed for short sale is your "hardship letter." A hardship letter is a letter addressed to the individual at the bank who will evaluate your request. At this stage, you may or may not have an individual assigned to you, but you will still prepare your paperwork at this stage.

The hardship letter is written to the signers on the mortgage explaining your situation and why both you and the bank will benefit from a short sale. The letter will describe how you got into your current financial position and show your desire to rectify the situation. The bank won't accept a short sale just because you'd like to move to another neighborhood, you're tired of your house, or you need more bedrooms. A short sale request must identify a *true* financial hardship in order to successfully negotiate an agreement with the bank. Here is an example of a successful hardship letter request:

SAMPLE HARDSHIP LETTER

October 1, 2012

ABC Bank
123 Main Street
Anywhere, USA

Attn: Short Sale Department
Re: Loan # 123456789

To Whom It May Concern:

We are formally requesting a short sale from your bank to settle our mortgage for an amount that is less than our current mortgage balance, to be paid in full and satisfied.

When we were originally approved for our mortgage five years ago, we were both fully employed with excellent credit; however, two years ago my husband became ill and could not work for several weeks. Although we had insurance, the co–pays and additional items that insurance would not cover were an expense that drained our savings account.

Due to my husband's lengthy absence, he lost his job and has been on unemployment benefits for the past year. His unemployment payments will cease in 60 days.

While I am still fully employed at my same place of employment, our income is not enough to cover the mortgage payments on a consistent basis, and we want to avoid foreclosure or declaring for bankruptcy protection.

We have explored all our options and have had a real estate agent review our property and provide us with a current Comparative Market Analysis to give us an idea of how much we could receive for our home were we to sell it.

The agent has determined that we could sell our home for $150,000 in a minimum of 90 days, probably longer. Our current mortgage balance is $250,000 and we do not have near the assets to pay off that note.

We are prepared to sell our home for $150,000 and request that you accept $150,000 as full and final payment to settle our current mortgage without future recourse.

We appreciate the opportunity to work with you to settle our mortgage debt with you quickly and permanently.

Sincerely,

Jane and John Doe
address
phone

cc: file, attorney, etc.

***

The bank will review your letter along with the rest of the short sale package. They may ask for additional documentation to be able to fully evaluate a possible short sale.

The bank will make a determination as to the current market value of your home. They can assess the value of your property by:

- The comparative market analysis provided by a real estate agent;

- An independent appraisal, or...

- A broker's price opinion (BPO).

A BPO is a written opinion by a licensed real estate agent that determines a current, approximate value.

If the value is in line with your short sale offer, the bank will ask for:

- Your most recent federal and state income tax returns;

- Your W–2s and 1099s;

- Bank and investment statements;

- Your most recent paycheck stubs;

- Profit and Loss Statements (from self–employed borrowers);

- An application and any other paperwork needed.

The bank will review your bank account statements and investment statements to see if there are any funds in your accounts that can go toward paying off the current mortgage. If there are, the bank might not accept your short sale offer of $150,000 and perhaps agree to a short sale of a slightly higher amount.

For instance, if you have $25,000 in your bank and you ask for a short sale payoff amount of $150,000 the bank might want you to pony up some or all of that $25,000 sitting in your checking account and accept a short sale amount of $175,000 instead. However, if you have little to no funds in your accounts, the bank will likely accept the offer you've made as the payoff amount.

The bank will review your pay stubs to confirm that your current income situation is as described in your hardship letter to verify that you have little opportunity of continuing to pay the mortgage balance in the near and long term. This goes back to showing that you are in "imminent default" and will soon have no ability to pay the mortgage and keep it current.

A bank will then evaluate its own situation regarding the property. Will the bank be better off by initiating the foreclosure process? Does the bank anticipate a bankruptcy filing, which wouldn't halt the foreclosure process in its entirety but simply delay the imminent foreclosure? Does the bank see that your current situation is temporary and will get better within the next 30 to 60 days?

When a bank forecloses on a home it's a very expensive process for it. It loses mortgage interest, back taxes that need to be paid, expensive legal fees that must be paid, and so on. Regardless of what the public might think, foreclosing on a property is not something a bank would like to see happen.

When the property becomes a non–performing asset. Even though the bank takes the asset (the house) back in a foreclosure, each month that the property sits in the bank's portfolio it costs the bank money. Too many non–performing assets and the feds can come knocking on the door, asking it to find some more cash reserves quickly. The bank then can face consequences, up to and including the loss of its banking license if unable to liquidate assets and move cash reserves into reserve accounts to cover foreclosure losses.

Okay, let's now say that the bank has accepted your short sale offer of $150,000 after review of your hardship letter, the comparative market analysis, and the documentation you provided. What next?

You sell the property to a buyer, obtain a contract, and close on the home. This time at the closing table you're on the seller's side, not the buyer's side. Do you sell the home by yourself or do you use a real estate agent? Let me give you a bit of advice: at this stage, you don't want to sell the home by yourself. You need to get your home listed in front of as many eyeballs as possible, and not just those in your neighborhood, but those investor eyeballs from across the country. To accomplish this daunting task you will most likely need a real estate agent to sell your home.

Secondly, do you want to be responsible for all the ins and outs of real estate documentation and paperwork? Realtors® learn how to cross every T and dot every I in the process of selling a home. They will have more experience than you will in negotiating a waiver of the deficiency judgment that you need. Any piece of this puzzle that goes missing can leave you vulnerable to paying the deficiency or moreover being sued for fraud if the sale is not legally processed. So again, when short selling your home, be prepared to do things the right way, and the way I know to ensure that is by using a licensed, bonded and experienced Realtor® that has experience on many short sale files. A good agent can provide you with testimonials and numbers of how many short sales they have processed and closed.

In fact, if you have a listing agreement signed by a real estate agent showing the list price of the home and present that agreement with your short sale request to the bank, the likelihood that your short sale offer will be accepted will be enhanced greatly. Further, if you have an offer from a buyer during your short sale request, your short sale request should be approved by the bank quicker if you already have a buyer and be accepted at a higher rate than without.

Short sales now comprise nearly 10 percent of all home sales in certain areas. In California, nearly one out of four homes sold is a short sale. In Nevada, it is nearly one out of every three homes sold. In fact, in both California and Nevada, states where I have worked extensively, short sales now outnumber foreclosures. This trend is growing across the country (Figure 7).

Figure 7: Short Sales Exceed Foreclosures January 2012, Data compiled from Bloomberg News, April 2012, http://www.bloomberg.com/news/2012-0417/short-sales-surpass-foreclosures-as-banks-agree-to-deals.html, retrieved March 2013.

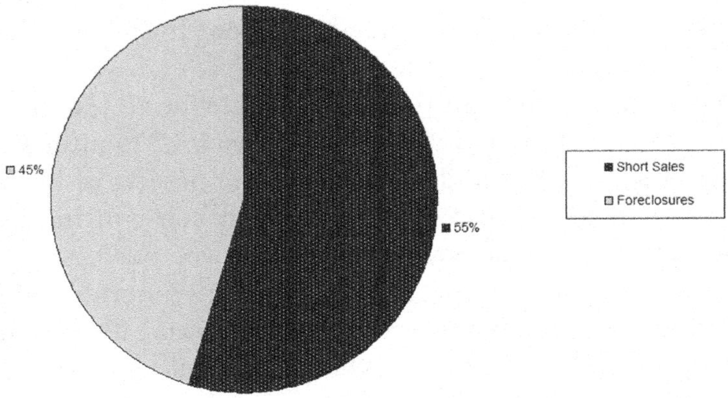

Getting your short sale request prepared in this manner—listed with a Realtor® and/or with a buyer offer—is without a doubt the strongest short sale offer you can make. Going further and including a buyer's Proof of Funds verification document, like a pre–approval letter or bank statement showing the funds in cash, will enhance the file still further. Banks are also getting the message—a lot of homeowners have just walked away from their homes dumping them on the banks' laps. Remember, when a bank forecloses:

1. The bank gets the property;
2. You may still be liable for the mortgage;
3. The bank adds the value of the property to its asset base.

With a short sale, it accepts less than the full mortgage balance and acknowledges the loan as paid in full and the property is completely off its books, having been sold to a third party. It is important that you ensure your short sale includes the verbiage that the loan is paid in full and the bank has no ability to pursue any deficiency at a later date.

The number of short sale transactions is up because banks have determined that it's an easy way to get rid of non–performing assets at a low cost. While a bank may make more money by re-selling the home in the future for a higher price, it must also evaluate the costs of holding onto the property during that term. The bank is not a property manager, they are not Realtors® and they certainly do not want to start predicting market trends and holding some homes and selling others. Banks want to lend money to people who will pay them back. Non-Performing assets are properties the bank has a mortgage or loan on where they are not receiving a monthly mortgage payment. Banks want as little non-performing assets in their portfolio as possible to be able to prove their financial solvency.

When you have an offer from a buyer, your real estate agent will evaluate the offer. This is where you need to have an experienced agent on your side. The agent will evaluate the creditworthiness of a buyer by way of reviewing a pre–approval letter from a bank on behalf of the buyer. Below is an example of a pre–approval letter.

PRE–APPROVAL LETTER

October 1, 2012

Joe Buyer
321 Main Street
Anywhere, Nevada

Mr. Buyer;

This is your letter of approval from ABC Bank. We have evaluated your loan application along with your credit reports, employment histories, and cash to close.
We have approved your mortgage loan application for a primary

residence or investment property for a loan amount not to exceed $500,000.

Sincerely,

Bank Loan Officer
ABC Bank

***

Once you have the approval letter along with a sales contract, your agent will submit the contract to the bank, open up an escrow account and you can expect to close within 30 or 90 days or so.

The buyer who has been approved for financing will wait for the bank to issue final approval. This will include reviewing the current title report and review of an acceptable, third–party appraisal. This appraisal will be separate and independent of any comparative market analysis or BPO. If all goes well, in about 30 days you will close on your property. You will be out from under the mortgage and you can begin your financial life anew without a foreclosure blemish on your record.

Finally, what is the best pre–approval letter that a buyer can present to you through your real estate agent? Perhaps it's no pre–approval whatsoever…it's a cash buyer. A cash buyer doesn't have to go through the appraisal and loan approval process that a bank will require. They only need to justify the price they are agreeing to buy the house at and show the cash in the form of verifying bank statements. When you see signs or letters from those who say they can buy your house and close within one week it's because they already have their financing lined up through a private lender or have money in the bank waiting to close.

Is a Short Sale Your Best Option?

Everyone's situation is going to be different. That's why this book objectively identifies all the positives and negatives associated with various options, such as foreclosure, deed–in–lieu, loan modifications, bankruptcies, and short sales.

However, in most cases, the benefits of a short sale, in my opinion, outweigh all other options:

- A foreclosure makes it more difficult to qualify for a mortgage than a short sale;
- Deficiency judgments are possible through a foreclosure, where with a short sale you're protected from further action while the Mortgage Debt Relief Act is still available to homeowners;
- Bankruptcies do not eliminate past debt, late payments, or your mortgage balance;
- Loan modifications are closest to a short sale in character, but you must still be able to qualify to pay the mortgage;
- Deed–in–lieu compared to a short sale still can leave you liable for past balances and will affect your credit with similar negativity to a foreclosure.

We'll review some scenarios in the next chapter that can help you decide which method might be best for you.

Chapter Eight

Similar Situations and Choices

The best we can do is size up the chances, calculate the risks involved, estimate our ability to deal with them, and then make our plans with confidence.

—Henry Ford

Dr. Jeanne

Jeanne graduated medical school on the West Coast in the mountains just a few hours from the coastal town she grew up in. After finishing her residency in a big East Coast city, she took a lucrative contract with a medical practice there—a position that made paying down the mountain of student loans she accumulated a distinct reality. She purchased a small two–bedroom house in the bustling city in 2006 after her first year of practice.

Although she loved her patients, Dr. Jeanne was having conflicts with the other doctors on staff. She couldn't get used to their gruff ways, their focus on the bottom line, their impersonal treatment style. In trying to cut corners, the doctors were operating more like accountants, spending more time on paperwork than with patients. She missed the laid–back, casual atmosphere of the West Coast. She missed her family. She started looking for a new job back where she felt she belonged.

It took nearly two years, but she finally found a spot in a practice in the same town where her family lived. The small town was a short walk to the ocean, a quick drive to the mountains. The other doctors gave of their time and shared her passion for service. They had a quality staff that handled all the administration and billing duties. From the moment she first visited the practice, she knew was among kindred spirits.

In 2011, Dr. Jeanne resigned from her East Coast medical practice and put her house up for a short sale. She lost about $65,000 as the house had gone underwater after the market collapsed in 2008. She decided that her happiness was worth that amount and sold the house at a short sale with no regrets. Fortunately, under the Mortgage Forgiveness Debt Relief Act, she was able to avoid paying taxes on the $65,000 "income" the bank had written off, though having to pay that tax wouldn't have changed her decision, as much of a hardship as it would have been.

Within two years, her credit recovered and she was able to buy the perfect small house near her family, her practice, and a beautiful river and wooded area. She is happy she made those choices and loves the new direction of her life.

***

This chapter will review sample financial profiles and review the pros and cons of the actions you choose. Most financial balance sheets will have all options available to them including foreclosure, loan modification, bankruptcies, deed–in–lieu, and short sales. Here we will examine sample balance sheets along with the impact of each choice.

We will first utilize the initial balance sheets mentioned in Chapter Three, Figure 5 on p. 39; Figure 8.

Assets		**Liabilities**	
Cash in Bank (Savings and Checking)	$3,000	Mortgage Loan Balance	$220,000
Stocks, Bonds, Mutual Funds	$2,000	Car Loan Balance	$5,250
Retirement Plans	$4,000	Credit Cards	$10,500
House Value	$150,000	Total Liabilities	$235,750
Automobile Value	$10,000		
Total Assets	$169,000	Net Worth (Assets – Liabilities) =	(–66,750)

Figure 8: Sample Balance Sheet

To review, this personal balance sheet shows a negative net worth of ($66,750) due to the underwater mortgage, and below we've added *Gross Monthly Income* on the asset side of the balance sheet and debts (expenses) on the Liabilities side. We've also included an additional three months past–due mortgage payments as a liability. In Figure 9 you will see a good example of a homeowner's situation that can lead to a successful short sale scenario.

Short Sale I

Assets		Liabilities	
Cash in Bank (Savings and Checking)	$3,000	Mortgage Loan Balance	$220,000
Stocks, Bonds, Mutual Funds	$2,000	Car Loan Balance	$ 5,250
Retirement Plans	$4,000	Credit Cards	$10,500
Gross Monthly Income	$5,000		
		Personal Debt Monthly Total =	$3,000
		–Housing (incl. taxes and insurance)	$1,800
		–Car Payment	$229
House Value	$150,000	–Other Monthly Expenses	$991
Automobile Value	$10,000		
		Past Due Mortgage (X3)	$7,500
		Total Liabilities	$246,250
		Net Worth (Assets – Liabilities)	
Total Assets	$169,000	$169,000 – $246,250 =	(–$77,250)

Figure 9: Sample Short Sale I Balance Sheet

This first example of a short sale is the simplest. The bank will evaluate the request and notice that your debt ratio represents 60 percent of your gross monthly income. This is exceptionally high, considering your monthly payments were always on time when you had two incomes. In this example, the bank would accept your short sale offer of $150,000, which is $70,000 less than the current mortgage balance. The bank will likely not pursue you for the $70,000 difference, and you are out from under your mortgage, ready to rebuild your financial life.

Short Sale II

Assets		Liabilities	
Cash in Bank (Savings and Checking)	$23,000	Mortgage Loan Balance	$220,000
Stocks, Bonds, Mutual Funds	$12,000	Car Loan Balance	$ 5,250
Retirement Plans	$4,000	Credit Cards	$10,500
Gross Monthly Income	$5,000	Personal Debt Monthly Total =	$3,000
		–Housing (incl. taxes and insurance)	$1,800
		–Car Payment	$229
House Value	$150,000	–Other Monthly Expenses	$991
Automobile Value	$10,000		
		Past Due Mortgage (X3 months)	$7,500
		Total Liabilities	$246,250
Total Assets	$199,000	Net Worth (Assets – Liabilities) =	
		$204,000 – $246,250 =	(–$42,250)

Figure 10: Sample Short Sale II Balance Sheet

Here you'll notice that the cash in bank and convertible stocks, bonds, and mutual funds total $35,000. Your income is the same at $5,000 per month, and your debt ratios are again high at 60 percent.

You present a short sale offer. The difference between the value of the home and the loan balance is $70,000. The bank sees that you have $35,000 in the bank in the form of liquid assets ($23,000 in Cash + $12,000 Stocks and Bonds not in a retirement account). The bank will likely refuse your short sale request in total or present a counteroffer.

In this example, a bank would not ask you to completely forfeit all of your assets to pay toward the loan balance but would ask you to contribute a certain amount, say $30,000. In this instance, the short sale request might be the current value of $150,000, less the $70,000 difference, plus your contribution of $30,000. The short sale amount agreed to by the bank would then be $180,000, representing your contribution plus the outstanding loan balance.

Loan Modification I

Assets		Liabilities	
Cash in Bank (Savings and Checking)	$3,000	Mortgage Loan Balance	$220,000
Stocks, Bonds, Mutual Funds	$2,000	Car Loan Balance	$5,250
Retirement Plans	$4,000	Credit Cards	$10,500
Gross Monthly Income	$5,000		
		Personal Debt Monthly Total =	$3,000
House Value	$150,000	–Housing (incl. taxes and insurance)	$1,699
Automobile Value	$10,000	–Car Payment	$229
		–Other Monthly Expenses	$1072
		Past Due Mortgage (X3 months)	$7,500
Total Assets	$169,000	Total Liabilities	$246,250
		Net Worth (Assets – Liabilities)	
		$174,000 – $246,250 =	(–$72,250)

Figure 11: Sample Loan Modification I Balance Sheet

Before your loan modification request is accepted by the bank, the bank will review your modification application and attempt to adjust your interest rate to the point where your monthly payment represents approximately 31 percent of your gross monthly income. In this example, the gross monthly income is $4,000. The bank will determine that your housing payment must be 31 percent of that amount, or $1,240 per month.

Your original loan balance was around $225,000 and you obtained a 30–year mortgage loan at 6 percent, with a principal and interest payment of $1,349. Adding monthly insurance and taxes of $350 makes your total housing payment $1,699 per month. When you were initially approved, (before loss of income/employment and hardship), your total monthly housing income was $6,000 and you had 37 percent debt ratio since your $1,699 PITIA payment + $521 additional monthly expenses = $2,220, and $2,220÷$6,000

= 37 percent DTI. Now the debt ratio is at 75 percent. That is \$3,000 ÷ \$4,000 (current income) = 75 percent.

Your lender will reduce your house payment ratio to 31 percent of the current \$4,000 income, or \$1,240. Subtracting the \$350 insurance and taxes leaves \$890 for a principal and interest payment. The lender will then determine that to get \$890 per month and a loan amount of \$220,000 on a 30–year mortgage your interest rate would need to be modified to approximately 2.68 percent.

In this example, the loan modification request would likely be considered, as the interest rate required is within range of current rates, but it must still be analyzed in comparison to additional monthly debt such as a car payment, utility bills, and other living expenses.

Loan Modification II

Assets		Liabilities	
Cash in Bank (Savings and Checking)	\$3,000	Mortgage Loan Balance	\$220,000
Stocks, Bonds, Mutual Funds	\$2,000	Car Loan Balance	\$ 5,250
Retirement Plans	\$4,000	Credit Cards	\$10,500
Gross Monthly Income	\$5,000		
		Personal Debt Monthly Total =	\$3,000
House Value	\$150,000	–Housing (incl. taxes and insurance)	\$1,800
Automobile Value	\$10,000	–Car Payment	\$229
		–Other Monthly Expenses	\$991
		Past Due Mortgage (X3 months)	\$7,500
Total Assets	\$169,000	Total Liabilities	\$246,250
		Net Worth (Assets – Liabilities)	
		\$174,000 – \$246,250 =	(–\$72,250)

Figure 12: Sample Loan Modification II Balance Sheet

In this example, the gross monthly income is $5,000 per month and your current debt ratio is 60 percent. Your lender will calculate your affordable housing payment using 31 percent of $5,000, or $1,550. With your current payment above this threshold at $1800 and 36 percent HTI, the underwriter will move forward trying to solve the equation and bringing the payment to affordability at 31 percent HTI (House Payment to Income Ratio).

Again, using a 30–year mortgage and a $220,000 loan amount, the lender's desired rate would then be just less than 1 percent, which is highly unlikely for a loan modification. In this case, a rate reduction is not sufficient to bring the loan to affordability. The second tool that the bank underwriter has is a mortgage balance reduction. If the current market value is $150,000, and the underwriter can reduce the balance to 110 percent of value, then the loan may be written down to $165,000. This may be enough to solve the affordability issue in itself. There may be no need to extend the term with that kind of balance reduction.

A new 30-year amortization at the same 6 percent paying on $165,000 would have a $990 payment before tax and insurance. In this case, the underwater mortgage would be addressed this way assuming the income could be verified at $4,000 monthly since $1,240 is affordable by the 31 percent ratio. With a principal and interest payment of $990, that leaves $250 for taxes and insurance, which would be about the right amount on a $150,000 home these days. This scenario could lead to a new lower mortgage and more affordable payment allowing the family to afford and stay in the home.

Be aware that even though the modified rate by the bank in this example is 5 percent, and even if market rates were 1 percent, the bank is not required to give you the best rate available in the market, only the rate required for getting your debt ratio in line. If the rate required to solve the problem is lower than available rates, then the next step is to look at a mortgage balance reduction, and then if that does not solve the problem, the term is extended one month at a time until the loan reaches affordability. If the maximum term extension does not bring the loan to affordability, then the loan is unaffordable compared to the verified income and the modification request is denied.

Banks will have their own internal guidelines when reviewing a loan modification request. Some banks will ask for a list of all monthly expenses, including outlays for food, utilities, clothing, and even dry cleaning bills, in some instances. Some banks take the size of the household and apply median averages for such expenses depending on the area. Some banks may also use different debt ratios to comply with their own internal guidelines, so your examples may vary.

When reviewing the loan modification option, the process is relatively simple, provided you supply the required documentation to your lender. Do not passively wait for a response. Follow up repeatedly to make sure the lender agrees that you submitted all the required documents. A diligent course of action is set to see the file through from start to finish requiring constant contact to fill any requests for further documentation or verbal verifications. Take notes of when you call—date and time, who you spoke to, and what you discussed. Rest assured that this is what the bank does; why should you be any different? A loan modification does not allow you any room to negotiate interest rates. The rates are set by bank regulators, and ***you do not have the legal right to contact other lenders for a loan modification; you must request a loan modification with the bank that has your loan.***

If your current income supports the acceptable debt–ratio limits established by the bank then a loan modification should be considered as a possible choice to help you navigate your foreclosure and underwater storm.

Bankruptcy

Assets		**Liabilities**	
Cash in Bank (Savings and Checking)	$3,000	Mortgage Loan Balance	$220,000
Stocks, Bonds, Mutual Funds	$2,000	Car Loan Balance	$ 5,250
Retirement Plans	$4,000	Credit Cards	$10,500
Gross Monthly Income	$5,000		
		Personal Debt Monthly Total =	$3,000
House Value	$150,000	–Housing (incl. taxes and insurance)	$1,800
Automobile Value	$10,000	–Car Payment	$229
		–Other Monthly Expenses	$991
		Past Due Mortgage (X3 months)	$7,500
Total Assets	$169,000	Total Liabilities	$246,250
		Net Worth (Assets – Liabilities)	
		$174,000 – $246,250 =	(–72,250)

Figure 13: Sample Bankruptcy I Balance Sheet

First, remember that a bankruptcy does not get rid of your current mortgage balance or your past–due mortgage payments. However, a bankruptcy can be helpful in that it can allow you to reduce your current credit obligations in order to increase your monthly cash flow, helping you to catch up on your mortgage.

If your gross monthly income allows you to file for a complete discharge of all dischargeable debts, then in this example you will discharge your automobile payment and have the ability to keep your automobile after the discharge. You must reaffirm the debt to keep the car. Reaffirming the debt means signing new loan documents, etc. If you wish to discharge the debt, you must relinquish the car. In addition, you will still need to pay the $7,500 outstanding mortgage payments outside of the bankruptcy.

If your income is such that you cannot file for a Chapter 7, you can file for a Chapter 13. In our example, that means you will spread your $229 monthly car payments and $7,500 past–due mortgage payments over a predetermined period from 36 to 60 months.

A Chapter 13 bankruptcy is an option for you if your current monthly income can support your current house payments but you're having problems getting caught up. A Chapter 7 does little unless you have a significant amount of monthly credit payments that you're currently paying.

If wiping out current credit obligations frees up enough monthly income to get caught up on a mortgage, then avoiding foreclosure by filing a bankruptcy is a possibility. If not, bankruptcies typically do very little, if anything, other than to buy time. It does not reduce your payments nor absolve your from your mortgage obligation.

Also, keep in mind that bankruptcy is a legal proceeding and that means legal fees. Legal fees are most always paid in advance before any bankruptcy can be filed, and they usually range around fifteen hundred dollars. Most attorneys, in order to remain competitively priced, will have similar fees to their peers.

Deed–in–Lieu

Instead of paying for the mortgage, you can offer to simply turn in the mortgage deed and return the property to the lender and avoid the foreclosure process.

Reviewing balance sheets for this situation is meaningless; all you're concerned with is the outcome. A lender won't necessarily review your financials in order to approve a deed–in–lieu, but it's certainly within their right.

If you've been relatively on time with your mortgage payments, a bank is likely to reject your request for deed in lieu of foreclosure. There's no reason for them to comply. A bank will consider a deed–in–lieu if they believe that there is no way for you to repay

your mortgage and you've provided evidence of the same.
A deed–in–lieu is the simplest of all options. You just walk away from the mortgage, but not from the outstanding mortgage balance or past–due payments. A bank can, in most instances, take you to court and sue for a deficiency judgment. If a bank takes your deed and then sells the property at below what you owe, the bank may see you in court in hopes that a deficiency judgment for the difference will be awarded. The bank can also send you an IRS1099–C form for the taxable year reflecting the difference on what you owed and what the bank sold the property for…you may be liable for additional income taxes.

See: Mortgage Relief Debt Act for more information on deficiency judgments. Additionally, it is important to note that lenders typically view a deed–in–lieu the same as a foreclosure when evaluating credit requests. In the bank's view, either way, foreclosure or deed–in–lieu means that they lose money and gain a property they do not want to own as they make no money on it while it sits empty and weighs on their books. The hit to your credit report will therefore be equivalent regardless of whether a foreclosure or a deed–in–lieu occurs. It is better to call your bank and work out a deed in lieu of foreclosure exchange as it shows effort on your part to resolve the issue, but it can have credit implications almost as bad as a foreclosure.

Foreclosure

This process, described in more detail in Chapter III, is the avenue that most homeowners fear: they lose the home, still owe the mortgage, and their credit is damaged more than just about any other option. Just as with a deed–in–lieu, foreclosure means potentially remaining liable for past–due amounts and deficiencies. A foreclosure is the worst case scenario for your credit report than any other single action.

Your options, in order of favorability are:

1. Short Sale;
2. Loan Modification;

3. Bankruptcy;
4. Deed–in–Lieu;
5. Foreclosure.

If you have the ability to successfully negotiate a short sale with your bank, then this is most always the best option for an underwater mortgage. It includes less paperwork and less impact on your credit report when compared with other options. For those who would really like to stay in their home, a loan modification would be their first option and could be tried before short selling. The paperwork needed for a loan modification is almost exactly the same as for a short sale, so many proceed with applying for a loan modification hoping for a solution. If the bank doesn't approve a workable deal for you, the owner, you can still put your property up for a short sale, assuming that you did not wait until the last minute before your assigned foreclosure sale date to start the modification review.

You may be thinking, "Hey, my credit is destroyed as it is...what do I care about damaging it further?" Your life will move on, and you will repair your credit. The sooner you can raise your credit scores to acceptable levels, the sooner you will be back on your feet. You want to make certain you make the best choice for you and your family with the options you have available at the time.

As you can see in the chart below, home sales, which dropped dramatically starting in 2007, are beginning to come back up.

Figure 14: Homes Sold from 2005 to 2012. Data Retrieved from US Census Bureau at http://www.census.gove/construction/nrs/historical_data/, retrieved March 2013.

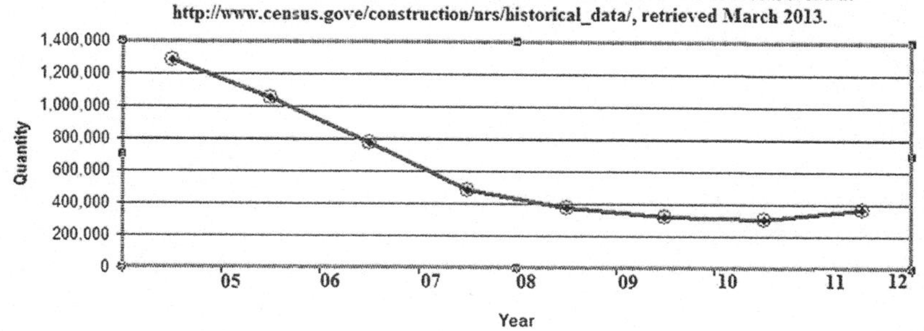

Whatever option you feel is best for you, be sure you are taking your future into account with all your decisions. During a financial crisis, it's easy to put your head down and just concentrate on getting through. Times will get better though, and the decisions you make today will affect you tomorrow, mostly in the form of your credit rating.

We'll explore how to repair and establish credit in the next chapter.

Chapter Nine

Six Ways to Save Your Credit from Drowning

An investment in knowledge always pays the best interest.

—Benjamin Franklin

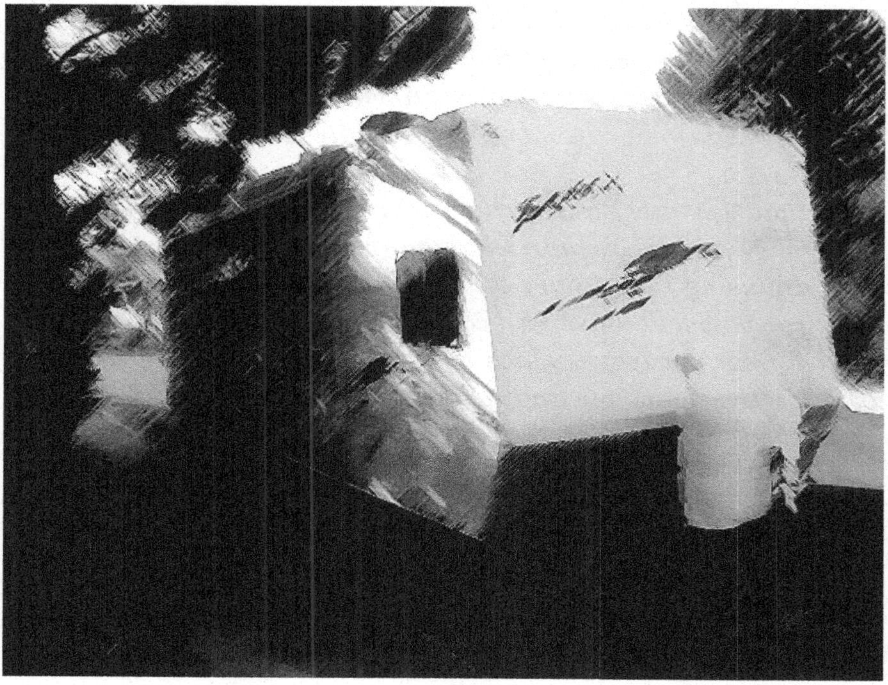

Kate and Ted

Kate and Ted, a young married couple with no children, just concluded a short sale on their underwater home and are now living in Kate's parents' motor home on the one–acre country lot where her parents' house stands. Lucky for them, Kate's parents have lots of room, the motor home is a pretty swank affair, and Ted has always gotten along with his in–laws. The young couple finds the arrangement just fine for now.

Kate and Ted had an adjustable rate mortgage that didn't adjust in their favor. At the five–year mark, the amount of their monthly mortgage payment nearly doubled while their income had remained nearly the same. Although they were both employed, there was no way they could absorb the added expense without added income, and they could see no way to add that much income.

They came close to foreclosure but managed to short sell before the foreclosure process was completed. The sale felt like a stroke of luck in a depressed neighborhood in a market during a recession. Having the weight of that mortgage lifted from their shoulders and the constant stress of imminent foreclosure removed from their lives has made the move to the country feel like an adventure.

Now that they don't have a huge mortgage that they can't afford, for a house worth less than what they paid for it six years previous, they are using that money to pay off their other debts, primarily their car payment and credit cards. They are taking the amount of their former mortgage, which was $2500, and splitting it equally between their car note and two credit cards—around $800 each. Once those are paid off, they'll start putting the former mortgage money to work paying off the remaining debts, and adding to savings and investments.

Kate and Ted hope to improve their credit score in the next two to five years, enough to purchase a more affordable home. Maybe something in the country. They are well on their way to achieving all their goals.

Bad credit happens to good people every single minute of every single day. You're not alone. While you may not exactly feel great about your situation, bad credit can be rehabilitated and repaired. But just like every other aspect of weathering these trying financial times, the key is information. Unless you know the components of a good credit score, you will spend much time on your credit profile with little improvement.

Credit scores range from 300 to 850, with 850 being the best credit and 300 the worst. Credit scores can come from a variety of credit reporting firms but the one lenders most use is called the FICO score, which stands for Fair Isaac Corporation, the company that invented the mortgage credit score algorithm.
Your FICO score is divided among five categories, each contributing to the overall score. These five categories are:

1. Payment History: 35 percent
2. Available Balances: 30 percent
3. Length of Time with Credit: 15 percent
4. Types of Credit: 10 percent
5. Credit Inquiries 10 percent

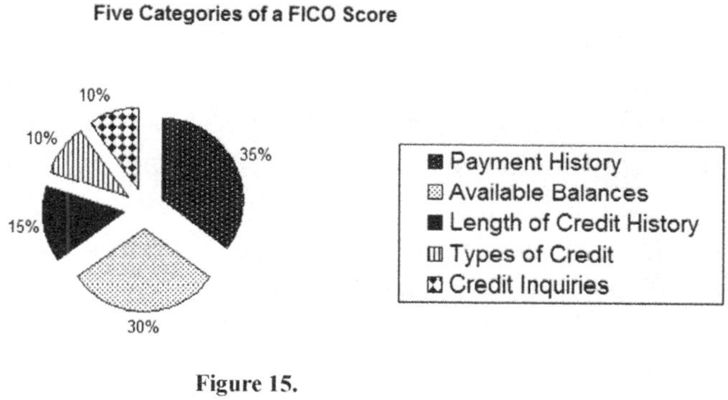

Figure 15.

Payment History

Your payment history is a result of your most recent credit payment patterns. *Most recent* refers to the credit activity within the past two years. Credit payments that are four, five, six years old or more matter little, if any. That's why a late payment last month will harm your credit score more than one that was made in 2005.

Payment history comprises 35 percent of your total credit score. Kate and Ted are wise to make on–time payments on their outstanding debts every month—in this way, when they are ready to buy another home; they'll have the good credit score necessary to help them get a good loan and at a good rate. Good credit has other benefits as well when considering any large purchase such as a car, and is especially beneficial if your job requires a good credit score. It's a win/win situation for borrowers and lenders.

If you make your monthly payments on time, your payment history will be perfect. If you make a payment that is more than 30 days past the due date, your credit score will drop. If you make a payment that is more than 60 days past the due date, your score will drop yet again and, if your payment is more than 90 days late, your score will drop even lower. This is important to note to help you navigate your financial storm. If you do anything to help your scores, payment history is of the utmost importance.

If your credit account goes into a collection status, your scores drop even lower. If the account goes to court and there is a judgment recorded against you, your scores will continue to fall.

If you file for a bankruptcy, your scores will fall further still. Continuing to make late payments afterward will drop it even more.

Finally, if there is a foreclosure on your credit report, your scores will drop to their lowest levels.

Available Balances

Available balances make up 30 percent of your score and the number is calculated by comparing the amount of credit you have available to you with your current credit balances. An ideal balance is approximately one–third of your credit line.

For example, you have two credit cards, each with a $10,000 credit limit for a total of $20,000. If you have nothing charged on either card, you have a zero–percent utilization. If you have a balance of $20,000 on a $20,000 limit, your utilization rate is 100 percent. If your balance is $30,000 and your limit is $20,000, your utilization rate is 150 percent.

The best balance for purposes of credit score in this example is one–third of $20,000 or approximately $6,600. Notice here that the ideal balance isn't a zero balance; it's a balance of one–third. This ratio shows that you use credit responsibly, when needed, and *do not* charge up your cards.

As your utilization rate exceeds one–third, your scores will begin to falter. As it approaches 50 percent, the scores will continue to fall. If you go over your limit, your scores in this category will be hardest hit.

Notice now that these first two categories make up 65 percent of your score. That's two–thirds. It pays to notice that if you ***concentrate on these two categories your scores will improve the fastest.***

Length of Time with Credit

This is a category you simply can't do much about other than to wait for time to pass. Those who have established a credit history longer than others have demonstrated their creditworthiness over a longer period of time. This category makes up 10 percent of your total score.

Someone who is 50-years-old and has never had any late payments will have a better score than someone who is 25-years-old and has never had any late payments.

Here also is the time factor when it comes to recent history. A credit score is more affected by recent actions compared to ones that occurred more than two years or longer prior to when the score is being calculated. A late payment five years prior will have little, if any, affect on a credit score as long as the credit history has been on time since then.

Types of Credit

For purposes of calculating credit score the type of credit refers to credit that has been approved and issued to you. This might be a gas station credit card, a Visa or MasterCard, a line of credit with your bank, a car loan, and so on. Mortgage credit is considered the highest–ranking of all credit issued, meaning timely mortgage payments will reward your score more than a gas station credit card from an oil company. Likewise, negative items on a mortgage will count more against you than late payments on a credit card.

Types of credit represent 10 percent of your score.

Other financial credit offers can come from finance agencies that help those people who need to re–establish their credit. Such loans might be car loans, at a higher interest rate, or higher interest rate credit cards with lower limits for people with bad or damaged credit. However, such credit extensions are often the only option for those who are re–establishing their credit histories. If you're going to open these types of credit accounts, remember to keep your balances at or below around one–third of your credit limit and pay before the due dates.

Inquiries

Credit inquiries make up 10 percent of your score and tally how many, if any, lenders have looked into your credit report for purposes of extending credit at your request. Several recent inquiries into your credit report will drop your score. For example, requesting credit for a car or credit card generally initiates a credit review from the lender to determine if they will approve your request and at what limit and interest rate. This inquiry would be considered initiated by you because you applied for credit from a lender.

Note that inquiries made by credit issuers that are not initiated by you do not count against your score. If you receive a credit offer in the mail it's likely the sender has reviewed your recent credit. Further, when you pull your own credit report for your personal review that does not count against you in the same manner. Again, authorized reviews of your credit history initiated by you when you request credit from a lender will count against you. For example, if you are shopping for a car, and you apply for credit from five different car dealers, that will be five credit inquiries and can drop your credit rating slightly despite no derogatory credit activity.

Dispute Letters

Finally, *dispute letters* written to the credit agencies disputing a credit claim will do little regarding your score. If there is a mistake on your report, by all means, get it fixed by working with the credit bureaus. Simply writing a letter is a waste of time.

You need a full game plan to right any wrongs on your credit history.

When you begin to establish or re–establish your credit history, first pull your credit report to search for any errors. Note any mistakes. Next, contact the company or bank in whose name you found the error. If you can prove to the bank or company involved that they are incorrect by providing a canceled check, credit card receipt, and/or a statement showing the debt was paid off, or other correspondence showing the debt was paid, then they may update the error and send the updated information to the credit bureau. You can also put comments on your credit report explaining why you disagree with a certain bit of information on your credit report. This may or may not assist you in gaining credit, but some lenders do look at the comments.To make a comment on your credit report, contact the credit-reporting agency directly at Experien.com, or call 1–888–397–3742. Or visit Equifax.com online, or call 1–800–685–1111 for a free copy of your credit report. Equifax handles reporting disputes via a form on their website. Lastly, TransUnion.com, or call 1–800–916–8800. Also, be prepared to provide any evidence or proof to support your dispute.

Another way to dispute a reporting error would be to contact the actual credit bureau that is showing the mistake and provide them proof of the error and have them update your credit report. Again, it can be done online at any of the above websites, or by contacting them by phone. They will tell you what they need from you.

Be aware, also, that although the Internet is filled with companies who offer to pull your credit report for you and monitor your scores for you, and while that's always an option you may wish to choose, you'll likely be solicited to pay for other credit and financial services from that company. Free credit reports are common bait used to get contact information in order to spam people with advertisements. I don't advise you one way or another in this regard, but to simply inform you that they will likely harvest your information to send you other offers.

The three main credit reporting bureaus, Equifax, Experian, and Transunion have established a website where you can access your credit reports once yearly for free at annualcreditreport.com. You don't need a third party to monitor your credit score.

Remember: make sure you pay your mortgage or rent on time, every time. Making timely payments helps your score more than anything else you do. The next best thing you can do (and this isn't an either/or situation) is to keep your current balances at about one–third of your available credit lines. Doing both—making timely payments and keeping balances low—will go a long way toward a good credit score.

Evaluate your own situation. Are you likely to default on future credit again? Do you have a history of charging things that you don't really need only to soon find yourself in financial hot water yet again? The Federal Trade Commission has collected information for you that can provide you with a list of credit counseling agencies that can help you identify the behaviors that may have caused you to get behind in your payments. Knowing yourself is absolutely essential to establish positive credit.

This is a good time to honestly evaluate and prioritize things in your life. Kate and Ted, after giving up the home they loved through a short sale, had an opportunity to change the path they were walking on. They had a detailed conversation about what was more important in their life. Were clothes more important than spending time together? Was a shiny new car that you could impress your friends with more important than having enough to eat? Were clipping coupons and eating at home more valuable in both actual cost savings, healthier meals, and time spent together than restaurant meals? Would going hiking in nature be as or more satisfying than tromping through the mall, looking for some thing to purchase and fill a hole in your heart? These are the types of honest conversations you need to have with yourself, your spouse, or anyone who makes financial decisions in your household. It's time to get real and prioritize.

Either establishing a solid credit profile or re–establishing a damaged one takes the exact same path: concentrate on the categories that most affect your scores and you'll find your scores back up to fighting weight…and a lot sooner than you would have imagined! You just have to prioritize and work diligently at it.

And Finally...

I realize this is a lot of information to absorb in a short time. Take each bit of information and apply it to your unique situation as needed, and ignore the rest. These are the tools that I've used, that work, for both my personal and business finances to get through my own financial storm and to help friends and family. I hope you find them helpful also.

There are other resources available out there; a simple Internet search may put you in touch with the right information, people or organizations in your area that are there to help you. Whatever you do, realize that you have choices; you are not backed into a corner with nowhere to go. There is help available.

My intention with this book is to help as many people as possible become educated regarding any real estate trouble that might be looming. I hope it will help you, and if you still have questions, don't hesitate to reach out to Help with Houses.

Wishing the very best for you and your family.

—*Anthony Biagi*

But Wait: What About the...

Shadow Inventory

Who knows what evil lurks in the hearts of men?
The Shadow knows!

—Radio Show, Comic Book and Movie Superhero, *The Shadow*

Cue the creepy music and the flashlight–under–the–chin special effects for *The Shadow*, da, da, daaa! but seriously, the shadow I want to discuss is about economics—shadow inventory—perhaps not as exciting nor dramatic as "evil lurk[ing] in the hearts of men," but it is still something that can have an impact on average Americans' financial and daily lives, in addition to the U.S. economy as a whole.

I'm inclined to believe that economics, like medicine, is an art, not a science. I believe the necessary evidence to support this lies in the volatile role that the so–called "shadow inventory" plays in the U.S. economy.

First, let me explain what shadow inventory is. Essentially, shadow inventory is REOs, or Real Estate Owned homes. These are homes that are currently undergoing foreclosure or have been foreclosed on by a bank or lender, and are being held in inventory by the bank and have not been placed on the market for sale. Banks are holding back on this release of inventory so as not to drop the price of homes by flooding the market and which could drop their return on investment (ROI), or the amount they could make on the sale of a property.

The Shadow Inventory market is both simple and difficult to fully understand. We cannot possibly know with complete accuracy how banks think or what they will do next. If they dump the shadow inventory into the market, supply and demand says price would go down with greater inventory. That is, if demand stayed the same. Do you see how this would create a renewed problem for the banks themselves? They are in control of how fast or slow they meet government regulators' timelines and they have the cash to pay fines if they do not meet requirements. For example, take a look at the May 2013 article by Jessica Silver–Greenburg in the *New York Times (http://dealbook.nytimes.com/2013/15/06/new-york-to-sue-bank-of-america-and-wells-fargo-over-settlement-violations/?smid=fb-share)..*

In the article, big banks are being held accountable for the regulations they have failed to comply with. If they make more money by not complying and paying fines, do you think they have an incentive to change their strategy?

It is dangerous to assume that this "shadow inventory" will be dumped on the market causing round two or three of the housing crisis. That would require the banks to go through the same process of more foreclosures, more underwater mortgages to reduce the balance on with modifications, more short sales and REO properties to fill the shadow inventory vaults again. Think about it! What would you do if you were the bank? Would you dump the entire inventory and play with the market that just foreclosed on more homes in a decade than any other time in history? Or, would you slowly meter the inventory making sure that there was just enough, or just too little, to stabilize the market?

I do not know what the answer is, and I surely do not know what the banks will do next. What I can count on is that there are homeowners just like you and me that need help, and they need the best help that is available. My mission is to make a place where homeowners can get that information, a place where homeowners can know their options, and make it a place where they feel comfortable coming to me and my organization and asking for help. Homeowners need something different in the future or they will repeat the foreclosure debacles of the past.

This example may help tell a true tale about how banks think. Let's just run through one hypothetical scenario: If a home was foreclosed on at $300,000...but the current appraised value is around $150,000, the bank may hold it in their REO inventory. If it is put up for sale at the current $150,000 market value, and all properties like it are marketed at the same time, the real estate market might be flooded with too many available homes for sale compared to demand. They could see the price of those homes drop to, let's say, $135,000 due to the overwhelming numbers of available properties. The bank's ROI would be reduced by 10 percent in that hypothetical example. Banks are in business to make money, not lose money.

According to which source you use, there are between 1.7 million and 10 million homes currently held off market as shadow inventory. Last year, in 2012, it was forecast by multiple reputable sources, that a large amount of shadow inventory would be put back on the market for sale in 2012–13, glutting a market that was still soft due to a lethargic economy struggling to recover.

Any large dump of inventory at one single time into the housing market may have a steamrolling effect over the mild demand for houses and could cause a return to dropping prices in what would then be called a "buyer's market."

But that hasn't happened. We are still struggling through a seller's market with tight inventory and steady or rising prices.

Shadow inventory appears to have dropped by almost 15 percent but housing prices have not fallen along with it. How did this happen? Savvy investors in large numbers, who had their eye on the real estate and mortgage industry, took the opportunity to swoop in and purchase homes for far less than what they had sold for in previous years in order to catch the best of the market. They were then able to eithert rent them out, fix them up and flip them for an increased price, or hold onto them and wait for the housing market to bump back up.

This unexpected increase in home sales, fueled by investors, despite the release of some shadow inventory, has increased home prices and now we have to be careful. There may be a soft decline to correct the investor fueled comeback. On the other hand, there may be support being shown for homes at these prices since investors are willing to hold them at these rates and rent many of them for the time being, or for the long haul. Exactly where the market will go, we can never tell. It will be dictated largely by how quickly or slowly the shadow inventory returns to the market. People who are underwater—owe more than their home is worth—are not free to purchase a new, lower priced home until they get rid of the burdensome, overvalued one they live in. They cannot enter the market until they do. And there are still a very large number of homeowners who are underwater.

The effect of this is that prices have gone up slightly as home prices rise due to the large number of investor purchases. Investor demand will diminish as it continues to rise as they like to buy low—there's a low ROI available if they buy overpriced homes, so potentially, home sales will begin to fall again, making this slight increase in home prices just a brief upward spike in the home sales market. Even if it does, it probably will not be sustained.

The other reason for the downturn in shadow inventory available for sale has been the National Mortgage Settlement between mortgage providers and 49 states' attorneys generals and which gives relief to homeowners through the modification of loans, in particular, modification or reduction in the principal amount of the mortgage. This has provided relief for homeowners underwater on their homes as well as those struggling to make their monthly mortgage payment.

This combination of modifications not only has reduced the number of REOs, or shadow inventory, but reduced the numbers of homes on the market for sale or short sale. Since there is no overabundance of homes for sale at rock bottom prices, the market has mostly stabilized for now; however, that could easily change if unseen forces that affect the real estate market come forward.

It is also *always* the time to do all the due diligence that the market, the recent credit crisis and homeownership requires. If you rush out and buy the first house that you think is pretty, I cannot guarantee that "now not is the time," but if you use all the lessons from the last decade and you find people that are doing good work, then you have an opportunity to learn how to buy a house correctly and benefit from the purchase for a long time. If you purchase a house because you have to have it and other people want it, you will pay a premium price and have a hard time renting it if you ever move on. If you look and look and find a diamond in the rough and you spend most of your money on the house, but you save some money to upgrade it once you own it, you may find you have more of what YOU want and may have an easier time renting or selling it when you move. Remember also, when you're ready to sell, that new homeowners want a blank slate that they can decorate or transform into their own "nest" that uniquely reflects them and their lifestyle. Think classic styles and timeless centerpieces. If you want to lose money, paint it zebra–striped. No one will keep it that way and you will lose in the value game.

In the final analysis, caution, information and knowledge when purchasing property are your safety nets: don't go out there on a real estate high wire without them.

My last point doesn't really have anything to do with the others, but rather is an offshoot of the great real estate collapse. It is an area I've found offers a huge opportunity for the right investors—investors like me. The recession and real estate collapse resulted in so many foreclosures that banks couldn't release all their inventory onto the market. If they did, it would have led to even further drops in value. The future is bright for all those that respond to the changes in the real estate market. I hope and pray this book has helped you to get closer to your goals of home ownership and financial freedom.

Common Real Estate and Lending Terms

Acceleration. A loan accelerates when it is paid off early, usually at the request or demand of the lender. An acceleration clause within a loan document explicitly states the steps that must be followed, but usually it applies to nonpayment, late payments, or the transfer of the property without the lender's permission.

Adjustable Rate Mortgage. An ARM is a loan program where the interest rate may change throughout the life of the loan. An ARM adjusts based on terms agreed to between the lender and the borrower, but typically it may only change once or twice a year.

Alternate Credit. Items you must pay each month but that won't appear on your credit report, such as your telephone bill, are considered alternate credit. In relation to mortgage loans, while such items aren't reported as installment or revolving credit, alternate credit can establish your ability and willingness to make consistent payments in a responsible manner. Sometimes called non-standard credit.

Amortization. Amortization is the length of time it takes for a loan to be fully paid off. It is one of the terms agreed upon at the outset of a loan. Amortized payments are due at regular intervals. Sometimes called a fully amortized loan. Amortization terms can vary, but generally accepted terms run in five–year increments, from 10 to 40 years.

Annual Percentage Rate. APR is the cost of money borrowed, expressed as a yearly percentage rate. It is not the same as your interest rate. The APR is an additional cost tacked on by lenders for the cost of doing the loan. It is usually less than .1 percent. It is a useful consumer tool to compare different lenders, but unfortunately it is often not used correctly. The APR can only work when comparing the same exact loan type from one lender to another.

Appraisable Asset. Any item whose value can be determined by a third party expert is an appraisable asset. For example, that car you want to sell is an appraisable asset. If the item can be appraised and then sold, then you can use those funds to buy a house.

Appraisal. An appraisal is a report that helps to determine the market value of a property. An appraisal can be done in various ways, generally as required by a lender, from simply driving by the property to ordering a full–blown inspection, complete with full–color photographs. Appraisals compare similar homes in the area to substantiate the value of the property in question.

Appraisal Management Company. An appraisal management company is an independent third party who receives appraisal orders from lenders or mortgage brokers, places the appraisal order, and manages the appraisal ordering and receiving process.

APR. *See* Annual Percentage Rate.

ARM. *See* Adjustable Rate Mortgage.

Assumable Mortgage. Homes sold with assumable mortgages let buyers take over the terms of the loan along with the house being sold. Assumable mortgages may be fully or non–qualifying assumable, meaning buyers take over the loan without being qualified or otherwise evaluated by the original lender. Qualifying assumable loans mean that while buyers may assume terms of the existing note, they must qualify all over again as if they were applying for a brand–new loan.

Automated Valuation Model. An AVM is an electronic method of evaluating a property's appraised value, done by scanning public records for recent home sales and other data in the subject property's neighborhood. Although not yet widely accepted as a replacement for full–blown appraisals, many in the industry expect AVMs to eventually replace traditional appraisals altogether.

AVM. *See* Automated Valuation Model.

Balloon Mortgage. A balloon mortgage is a type of mortgage where the remaining balance must be paid in full at the end of a preset term. A five–year balloon mortgage might be amortized over a 30–year period, but the remaining balance is due, in full, at the end of five years.

Bridge Loan. A short–term loan primarily used to pull equity out of one property for a down payment on another is a bridge loan. This loan is paid off when the original property sells. Since such loans are short–term, sometimes lasting just a few weeks, usually only retail banks offer them. Usually the borrower doesn't make any monthly payments and only pays off the loan when the property sells.

Buydown. Paying more money to get a lower interest rate is called a *permanent* buydown, and it is used in conjunction with discount points. The more points, the lower the rate. A *temporary* buydown is a fixed–rate mortgage that starts at a reduced rate for the first period, and then gradually increases to its final note rate. A temporary buydown for two years is called a 2–1 buydown. For three years it's called a 3–2–1 buydown.

Cash–Out. A refinance mortgage that involves taking equity out of a home in the form of cash during a refinance is called a cash–out. Instead of just reducing the interest rate during a refinance and financing the closing costs, the borrower finances even more, putting the additional money in their pocket.

Closer. The closer is the person who helps prepare the lender's closing documents. The closer forwards those documents to the buyer's settlement agent's office, where the buyer will be signing closing papers. In other states, a closer can be the person who holds the loan closing.

Closing Costs. The various fees involved when buying a home or obtaining a mortgage are collectively called closing costs. The fees, required to issue a good loan, can come directly from the lender or may come from others in the transactions.

Collateral. Collateral is property owned by the borrower that's pledged to the lender as security in case the loan goes bad. A lender makes a mortgage with the house as collateral.

Comparable Sales. Comparable sales are that part of an appraisal report that list recent transfers of similar properties in the immediate vicinity of the house being bought. Also called "comps."

Conforming Loan. A conventional conforming loan is a Fannie Mae or Freddie Mac loan that is equal to or less than the maximum allowable loan limits established by Fannie and Freddie. These limits are changed annually.

Conventional Loan. A conventional loan is one that uses guidelines established by Fannie Mae or Freddie Mac and is issued and guaranteed by lenders.

Credit Report. A credit report is a document comprised of the credit extended to a consumer, their payment history, and also the individual's property addresses and any public records filed with any government agency, for example, a judgment against you.

Credit Repository. A credit repository is a place where credit histories are stored. Merchants and banks agree to store consumers' credit patterns in a central data bank that other merchants and banks can access.

Credit Score. A credit score is a number derived from a consumer's credit history and based upon various credit details in a consumer's past and upon the likelihood of loan default. Different credit patterns are assigned different numbers and different credit activity may have greater or lesser impact on the score. The higher the credit score, the better the credit.

Debt Consolidation. Paying off all or part of one's consumer debt with equity from a home results in debt consolidation. Debit consolidation can be part of a refinanced mortgage or a separate equity loan.

Debt Ratio. Debt ratio is gross monthly payments divided by gross monthly income, expressed as a percentage. There are typically two debt ratios to be considered: The *housing ratio*—sometimes called the front–end or front ratio—is the total monthly house payment, plus any monthly tax, insurance, private mortgage insurance, or homeowner's association dues, divided by gross monthly income. The *total debt ratio*—also called the back–end or back ratio—is the total housing payment plus other monthly consumer installment or revolving debt, also expressed as a percentage. Loan debt ratio guidelines are usually denoted as 32/38, with 32 being the front ratio and the 38 being the back ratio. Ratio guidelines can vary from loan to loan and lender to lender.

Deed. A deed is a written document evidencing each transfer of ownership in a property.

Deed–in–Lieu. Deed–in–lieu is an abbreviated term for "deed in lieu of a foreclosure." A deed–in–lieu is accomplished by the borrower, who transfers all interest in the subject property to the lender.

Deed of Trust: A deed of trust is a written document giving an interest in the home being bought to a third party, usually the lender, as security to the lender.

Deficiency Judgment. If you are foreclosed on and the lender then sold the home for less than the balance of the loan that you owed, depending on the nature of your note, your lender may obtain a judgment against you hoping to recover the remaining balance on your old mortgage from you.

Delinquent. Being behind on a mortgage payment is being delinquent. Delinquencies typically are recognized as 30+ days delinquent, 60+ days delinquent and 90+ days delinquent.

Discount Points. Also called "points," discount points are represented as a percentage of a loan amount. One point equals one percent of a loan balance. Borrowers pay discount points to reduce the interest rate for a mortgage. Typically each discount point paid reduces the interest rate by .25 percent, or one quarter. It is a form of prepaid interest to a lender.

Document Stamp. A document stamp is evidence—usually with an ink stamp—of how much tax was paid upon transfer of ownership of property. Certain states call it a *doc stamp*. Doc stamp tax rates can vary based upon locale, and not all states have doc stamps.

Down Payment. A down payment is the amount of money initially given by the borrower to close a mortgage. The down payment equals the sales price less financing. It's the very first bit of equity a buyer will have in a new home.

Easement. An easement is a right of way previously established by a third party. Easement types can vary but typically involve the right of a public utility to cross an owner's land to access an electrical line.

Equity. Equity is the difference between the appraised value of a home and any outstanding loans recorded against the house.

Escrow. Depending upon where you live, escrow can mean two things. On the West Coast, for example, when a home goes under contract it "goes into escrow" (*see also* Escrow Agent). In other parts of the country, an escrow is a financial account set up by a lender to collect monthly installments for annual tax bills and/or hazard insurance policy renewals.

Escrow Account. *See* Impound Account.

Escrow Agent. On the West Coast, the escrow agent is the person or company that handles the home closing, ensuring documents are assigned correctly and property transfer has legitimately changed hands.

FACTA. *See* Fair and Accurate Credit Transactions Act.

Fair and Accurate Credit Transactions Act. The FACTA is

a new law that replaces the Fair Credit Reporting Act, or FCRA, and governs how consumer information can be stored, shared, and monitored for privacy and accuracy.

Fair Credit Reporting Act. The FCRA was the first consumer law that emphasized consumer rights and protections relating to their credit reports, their credit applications, and privacy concerns.

Fannie Mae. *See* Federal National Mortgage Association.

FCRA. *See* Fair Credit Reporting Act.

Fed. The Fed is the shorthand name for the Federal Reserve Bank.

Fed Funds Rate. The Fed funds rate is the rate banks charge one another to borrow money overnight.

Federal Home Loan Mortgage Corporation. The FHLMC, or Freddie Mac, is a corporation established by the U.S. government in 1968 to buy mortgages from lenders made under Freddie Mac guidelines and is owned by the Federal Government.

Federal Housing Administration. The FHA was formed in 1934 and is now a division of the Federal Housing Finance Agency (FHFA). It provides loan guarantees to lenders who make loans under FHA guidelines.

Federal Housing Finance Agency. The FHFA was established as the result of the Housing and Economic Recovery Act of 2008. This agency controls Fannie Mae, Freddie Mac, HUD, and the Federal Home Loan Banks.

Federal National Mortgage Association. The FNMA, or Fannie Mae, was originally established in 1938 by the U.S. government to buy FHA mortgages and provide liquidity in the mortgage marketplace. It is similar in function to Freddie Mac. In 1968, its charter was changed, and it now purchases conventional mortgages as well as government ones.

Federal Reserve Board. The Federal Reserve Board is the head of the Federal Reserve Banks that, among other things, sets overnight lending rates for banking institutions. The Fed does not set mortgage rates.

FHA. *See* Federal Housing Administration.

FICO. FICO stands for Fair Isaac Corporation, the company that invented the most widely used credit scoring system.

Final Inspection. Final inspection is the last inspection of a property, showing that a new home being built is 100 percent complete or that a home improvement is 100 percent complete. It lets lenders know that their collateral and their loan are exactly where they should be.

Fixed Rate Mortgage. A fixed rate mortgage is a loan whose interest rate does not change throughout the term of the loan.

Flood Certificate. A flood certificate shows whether a property or part of a property lies above or below any local flood zones. These flood zones are mapped over the course of several years by the Federal Emergency Management Agency (FEMA). The certificate identifies the property's exact legal location and a flood line's elevation. There is a box that simply asks, "Is the property in a flood zone, yes or no?" If the property is in a flood zone, the lender will require special flood insurance that is not usually carried under a standard homeowner's hazard insurance policy.

Foreclosure. A foreclosure is the bad thing that happens when the mortgage isn't repaid. Lenders begin the process of forcefully recovering their collateral when borrowers fail to make loan payments. The lender takes the house away.

Freddie Mac. *See* Federal Home Loan Mortgage Corporation.

Gift. When the down payment and closing costs for a home are given to the borrower instead of the funds coming from their own accounts, it is called a gift. Usually such gifts can only come from family members or foundations established to help new homeowners.

Gift Affidavit. A gift affidavit is a form signed whereby someone swears that the money they're giving is indeed a gift, not a loan, and is to be used for the purchase of a home. Lenders like to see that form, as well as a paper trail of the gift funds being added to a person's own funds.

Gift Funds. Gift funds are monies given to a borrower for the sole purpose of buying a home. These funds are not to be paid back in any form and are usually given by a family member or a qualified nonprofit organization.

Government National Mortgage Association. The GNMA, or Ginnie Mae, is a U.S. government corporation formed to purchase government loans like VA and FHA loans from banks and mortgage lenders.

Good Faith Estimate. A list of estimated closing costs on a particular mortgage transaction is, collectively, a good faith estimate. This estimate must be provided to the loan applicants within 72 hours after receipt of a mortgage application by the lender or broker or immediately if the application is taken face–to–face.

Hazard Insurance. A specific type of insurance that covers against certain destructive elements such as fire, wind, and hail. It is usually an addition to homeowners insurance, but every home loan has a hazard rider.

HELOC. *See* Home Equity Line of Credit.

Home Equity Line of Credit. HELOC is a credit line using a home as collateral. Customers write checks on this line of credit whenever they need to and pay only on balances withdrawn. It is much like a credit card, but secured by the property.

Homeowners Insurance. An insurance policy that covers not just hazard items, but also other things, such as liability or personal property.

Home Valuation Code of Conduct. HVCC was established as a national lending rule that prohibits lenders or mortgage brokers from influencing property values by communicating directly with an appraiser. It provides rules for ordering, compensating, and selecting an appraiser.

Imminent Default. Term used to describe the severity to which the homeowner is progressing through foreclosure.

Impound Account. An impound account is set up by a lender to deposit a monthly portion of annual property taxes or hazard insurance. As taxes or insurance come up for renewal, the lender pays the bill using these funds. Also called an *escrow account.*

Inspection. An inspection is a structural review of the house to determine defects in workmanship, damage to the property, or required maintenance. An inspection does not determine value of the property. There are different kinds of inspections. A pest inspection, for example, looks for termites or wood ants.

Installment Account. Borrowing a lump sum and agreeing to pay it back a certain amount each month—in installments—until the loan is paid off. For example, a car loan with a monthly payment for a set amount of time is an installment account.

Interest Rate. An interest rate is the amount charged to borrowed money over a specified period of time.

Interest Rate Reduction Loan. An IRRL is a VA refinance loan program that has relaxed credit guidelines. Also called a *streamline refinance.*

IRRL. *See* Interest Rate Reduction Loan.

Jumbo Loan. A mortgage that exceeds current conforming loan limits is called a jumbo loan.

Junior Lien. A second mortgage or one that subordinates to another loan is a junior lien. This is not as common a term as it used to be. You're more likely to hear the terms *second mortgage* or *piggyback* these days.

Land Contract. An arrangement where the buyer makes monthly payments to the seller but the ownership of the property does not change hands until the loan is paid in full is a land contract.

Land–to–Value. An appraisal term that calculates the value of the land as a percentage of the total value of the home is called land–to–value. If the land exceeds the value of the home it's more difficult to find financing without good comparable sales. Also called lot–to–value.

Lease–Purchase Agreement. Also known as rent–to–own, a lease–purchase agreement is an option whereby a buyer leases a home until the buyer has saved up enough money for down payment to qualify for a conventional mortgage.

Lender Policy. Title insurance that protects a mortgage from defects or previous claims of ownership is a lender policy.

Liability. An obligation or bill—a debt—on the part of the borrower is a liability. It works like an automobile loan. When you pay off the car, you get the title. Liabilities such as student loans or a car payment can show up on a credit report, but they can also be anything else that you are obligated to pay. Those liabilities on the credit report are used to determine debt ratios.

Lien. A lien is a legal claim or prior interest on a property that is about to be bought. A lien is a legal right to security interest in a property in order to ensure payment of a loan or debt levied against it. This can be a home or a piece of personal property. A lien is the reflection of a debt that is owed on a particular piece of property that was used for collateral for the loan. It is always wise to check for liens, which would pass on to the new buyer, prior to buying any property.

Loan. Money granted to one party with the expectation of it being repaid is a loan.

Loan Officer. A loan officer is typically responsible for helping mortgage applicants get qualified and assisting in loan selection and loan application. Loan officers can work at banks, credit unions, mortgage brokerage houses, or for bankers.

Loan Processor. Loan processors gather the required documentation for loan applications for loan submission. Along with the loan officer, a buyer will work with the loan processor quite a bit during the mortgage process.

Loan Underwriter. The loan underwriter is responsible for ultimately saying "yes" or "no" on a loan file. The underwriter compares loan guidelines with what the potential buyer has documented in the file.

Loan–to–Value Ratio. LTV is expressed as a percentage of the loan amount when compared to the valuation of the home determined by an appraisal. If a home was appraised at $100,000 and the loan amount was $70,000, then the LTV would be 70 percent.

LTV. *See* Loan–to–Value Ratio.

Market Value. In an open market, the market value of a property is both the highest the borrower is willing to pay and the least the seller is willing to accept at the time of contract. Property appraisals help justify market value by comparing similar home sales in the subject property's neighborhood.

Mortgage. A loan with the property being pledged as collateral is a mortgage. The mortgage is retired when the loan is paid in full.

Mortgage Brokers. Companies that set up a home loan between a banker and a borrower are mortgage brokers. Brokers don't have money to lend directly, but they have experience in finding various loan programs that can suit the borrower, similar to how an independent insurance agent operates. Brokers don't work for the borrower but instead provide mortgage loan choices from other mortgage lenders.

Mortgagee. A mortgagee is the person or business making the loan; also called the lender.

Mortgagor. A mortgagor is the person(s) getting the loan; also called the borrower.

Multiple Listing Service. MLS is a central repository where real estate brokers and agents show homes and search for homes that are for sale.

Nonconforming. Nonconforming loans are those whose amounts are above current Fannie or Freddie limits. *See also* Jumbo Loan.

Note. A note is a promise to repay. It may or may not have property involved and may or may not be a mortgage.

Note Modification. A note modification is a process where a mortgage lender modifies the current structure of the outstanding note, often to assist a borrower who may be having difficulties making their regular mortgage payment as reflected by the original note.

Notice of Default. NOD is delivered by Certified Letter from the mortgage lender to the borrower when two successive mortgage payments have been missed. A legal process filing, the NOD becomes a public record, recorded in the county or parish where the property resides.

Origination Fee. The origination fee is charged to cover costs associated with finding, documenting, and preparing a mortgage application and is usually expressed as a percentage of the loan amount.

Owner's Policy. An owner's policy is title insurance made for the benefit of the homeowner.

Payment Shock. Payment shock is a term used by lenders referring to the percentage difference between what a borrower is paying for housing at a current time and what a new payment would be under an adjustable rate mortgage. Most loan programs don't have a payment shock provision, but for those that do, a common percentage increase is 150 percent.

PITI[A]. Principal, Interest, Taxes, and Insurance and sometimes Association Fees, are figures used to help determine front debt ratios. In condos, townhouses, or co–ops HOA dues replace the payment for insurance.

Portfolio Loan. A portfolio loan is made by a direct lender, usually a bank, and kept in the lender's loan portfolio instead of being sold or underwritten to any external guidelines.

Pre–foreclosure. A pre–foreclosure is a property where foreclosure is imminent. It is often associated with an impending or current Notice of Default, or NOD.

Prepaid Interest. Daily interest collected from the day of loan closing to the first of the following month is prepaid interest.

Principal. The outstanding amount owed on a loan, not including any interest due, is the principal.

Quit Claim. A quit claim is a release of any interest in a property from one party to another. A quit claim does not, however, release the obligation on the mortgage.

Rate–and–Term Refinance. Refinancing to get a new rate is rate–and–term refinancing. The borrower is changing the interest rate and changing the term, or length, of the new note. This process requires a full approval process exactly as the purchase loan was issued.

Realtor®. A Realtor® is a member of the National Association of Realtors and a registered trademark. Not all real estate agents are Realtor®.

Recast. Recast is a term applied to ARMs and used when extra payments are made to the principal balance. When a note is recast, the monthly payment is calculated for the borrower.

Refinance. Obtaining a new mortgage to replace an existing one is refinancing. There is also a rate–and–term refinance, where only the outstanding principal balance, interest due, and closing costs are included in the loan.

Reissue. When refinancing, there may be discounts if the same title agency is used. The reissue of an original title report can cost much less than a full title insurance policy.

Recission. Withdrawal from a mortgage agreement is rescission. Refinanced mortgage loans for a primary residence have a required three–day "cooling off" period before the loan becomes official. If for any reason the buyer decides not to take the mortgage, that person can "rescind" and the whole deal's off.

Reserves. A borrower's assets after closing are the reserves. Reserves can include cash in the bank, stocks, mutual funds, retirement accounts, IRA's, and 401 (k) accounts.

Revolving Account. A credit card or department store account on which there is typically a limit and the consumer doesn't make any payments until they charge something is called a revolving account.

Sales Contract. A sales contract is a written agreement to sell or purchase a home, signed by both the seller and buyer.

Second Mortgage. Sometimes called a "piggyback" mortgage, a second mortgage assumes a subordinate position behind a first mortgage. If the home goes into foreclosure, the first mortgage would be settled before the second could lay claim. See also Junior Lien.

Seller. The person transferring ownership and all rights for a home in exchange for cash or trade is the seller.

Settlement Statement. Also called the Final HUD–1, the settlement statement shows all financial entries during the home sale, including sales price, closing costs, loan amounts, and property taxes. The initial good faith estimate will be the first glimpse of the settlement statement. This statement is one of the final documents put together before the closing and is prepared by the buyer's attorney or settlement agent.

Short Sale. A short sale is when a property changes hands from seller to buyer, the lender has agreed to accept less for their outstanding mortgage note than the current balance or payoff amount, and the seller is released from all future obligation to repay the mortgage and any delinquent amounts.

Survey. A map that shows the physical location of the structure and where it sits on the property is a survey. A survey also designates any easements that run across or through the property.

Title Insurance. Title insurance is protection for the lender, the seller, and/or the borrower against any defects or previous claims to the property being transferred or sold.

Title. Title is legal ownership in a property.

Title Exam/Title Search. The process where public records are reviewed to research any previous liens on the property is a title exam or title search.

Underwater Mortgage. An underwater mortgage is a piece of leveraged real estate where the mortgage balance exceeds the current property value.

VA Loan. A VA loan is a government mortgage guaranteed by the Department of Veterans Affairs.

VA No–No. A VA No–No is a type of VA loan where the borrower not only puts no money down, but also pays no closing costs.

Verification of Deposit. A VOD is a form mailed to a bank or credit union that asks the institution to verify that a borrower's bank account exists, how much is in it, how long the borrower has had it, and what the average balance was over the previous two months.

VOD. *See* Verification of Deposit.

Wraparound Mortgage. A wraparound mortgage is a method of financing where the borrower pays the former owner of the property each month in the form of a mortgage payment. The former owner will then make a mortgage payment to the original mortgage holder. This is not allowed without the initial lender's permission.

Worksheet

Asset and Liability Worksheet, i.e., Balance Sheet

Assets	$ Amount	Liabilities	$ Amount
Cash in Bank (Savings and Checking)		Mortgage Loan Balance	
Stocks, Bonds, Mutual Funds		Car Loan Balance	
Retirement Plans		Medical Bills	
House Value		Other Bills	
Other Assets			
Total Assets		**Total Liabilities**	
		Net Worth [Assets - Liabilities =]	

ABOUT THE AUTHOR

(Jeramie Lu Photography, 2013)

Anthony Biagi has been helping people achieve their dreams for decades by providing financial and life advice to clients who have gone on to establish successful businesses, build financial freedom, and create improved quality of life.

Over the last 10 years, Anthony has been intimately involved in the real estate market and seen up close the overwhelming role the sub-prime loan crisis has played in rocking the U.S. economy. From his work as a real estate investor to his experience of going through foreclosure, his education transcends what he learned in college.

Anthony's new company, ***Help with Houses***, uses the principles acquired through *Rich Dad Education* and a lifetime of paying attention to how money works. ***Help with Houses*** focuses on helping people solve their mortgage problems as well as anything in relation to real estate, including buying or selling.. In addition, they help people learn the successful and proven strategies for home ownership and real estate investing.

Help with Houses has implemented proven strategies for success including: Property Management Techniques, Property Acquisition Strategies, Property Flips, Long Term Hold Evaluation, Rehabilitation and Resale Projects, and a Lease with Option Program designed to help potential buyers with less than perfect credit.

Meanwhile, his most important project in life is watching his 3–year–old daughter learn how to swim with her first swimming lessons, seeing how high she can jump at her gymnastics class, and just being able to sit back, relax, and read her stories.

If you'd like to contact Anthony, you may at any of the below:

Anthony Biagi:

HelpwithHouses.com

Local: 775-393-9478

Toll Free: 855-435-7969

E-mail: Info@helpwithhouses.com

Twitter: @HelpwithHouses

Facebook: https://www.facebook.com/HelpWithHouses

https://www.facebook.com/pages/The-Homeowner-Blueprint-Navigating-the-Real-Estate-Storm/365460893557362

Linkedin: http://www.linkedin.com/pub/anthony-biagi/50/994/988

YouTube Channel: http://www.youtube.com/channel/UCZfJ0odoIoFAP265np7OX9A

References

"CoreLogic Reports 69,000 Completed Foreclosures Nationally in March," Core Logic, last modified May 1, 2012, accessed February 28, 2013, corelogic.com/about–us/news/corelogic–reports–69,000–completed–foreclosures–nationally–in–march.aspx. \

"The Housing Crash and Smart Growth," The National Center for Policy Analysis, June 2011, accessed May 30, 2013, http://www.ncpa.org/pdfs/st335.pdf.

"Debt Stress Causing Health Problems, Poll Finds: Economic woes a pain in the neck, back, and more for millions of Americans," NBCNews.com, 2013, accessed May 30, 2013, http://www.nbcnews.com/id/25060719/

"Foreclosure Foul-up: Tracking Down Those 'Lost' Mortgages," *Time Magazine*, November 29, 2010, accessed May 30, 2013, http://www.time.com/time/magazine/article/0,9171,2032110,00.html

Silver-Greenberg, Jessica, "Two Big Banks Face Suits in Mortgage Pact Abuses," *The New York Times,* May 6, 2013, accessed May 30, 2013, http://dealbook.nytimes.com/2013/05/06/new-york-to-sue-bank-of-america-and-wells-fargo-over-settlement-violations/?smid=fb-share

Tracy, Joseph and Joshua Wright. "Payment Changes and Default Risk: The Impact of Refinancing on Expected Credit Losses." *Federal Reserve Bank of New York Staff Reports, no. 562*. Federal Reserve Bank of New York. New York, 2012 June.

"State Foreclosure Rate Report Q1–2009," Trulia.com, last modified May 12, 2009, accessed March 1, 2013, http://www.trulia.com/blog/loanmodexpert/2009/05/ state_foreclosure_rate_

"Median and Average Sales Prices of New Homes in United States," U.S. Census Bureau, last modified April, 2013, accessed May 30, 2013, http://www.census.gov/construction/nrs/pdf/uspricemon.pdf.

"Labor Force Statistics from the Current Population Survey: Unemployment Rate," United States Department of Labor, Bureau of Labor Statistics, last accessed February 28, 2013, data.bls.gov/timeseries/LNS14000000.

Welsh, Ian. "The Housing Bubble was Based on Fraud," June 26, 2010, accessed May 30, 2013, http://www.ianwelsh.net/2010/06/.

Sources

http://banking.about.com/od/mortgages/a/mortgagecrisis.htm

http://business.time.com/2013/01/22/what–ever–happened–to–the–big–bad–shadow–inventory–of–homes/

http://dacula.patch.com/blog_posts/wondering–how–shadow–inventory–will–impact–housing–in–2013

http://www.dsnews.com/articles/lack–of–inventory–not–shadow–is–real–concern–2013–02–22

http://www.economist.com/node/13145396?story_id=13145396

http://www.economist.com/node/9972489?story_id=9972489

http://www.forbes.com/sites/afontevecchia/2012/06/26/10–million–underwater–mortgages–and–shadow–inventory–worth–246b–mean–housing–trouble/

http://www.freddiemac.com/singlefamily/preventfraud/

http://www.investopedia.com/articles/07/subprime–overview.asp

http://www.jaxlawcenter.com/lawyer–attorney–1292539.html

http://www.mbaa.org/NewsandMedia/PressCenter/64769.htm

http://mortgage–home–loan–bank–fraud.com/articles/stop_foreclosure.htm

http://dealbook.nytimes.com/2013/05/06/new–york–to–sue–bank–of–america–and–wells–fargo–over–settlement–violations/?smid=fb–share

http://www.nolo.com/legal–encyclopedia/free–books/foreclosure–book/chapter9–3.html

http://www.realtytrac.com/content/press–releases/us–foreclosure–activity–increases–75–percent–in–2007–3604?accnt=64847

http://www.realtytrac.com/content/press–releases/foreclosure–activity–increases–81–percent–in–2008–4551?accnt=64847

http://useconomy.about.com/od/economicindicators/tp/Subprime–Mortgage–Primer.htm

http://www.washingtonpost.com/wp–dyn/content/article/2006/01/04/AR2006010402016.html

https://en.wikipedia.org/wiki/Subprime_mortgage_crisis

http://wsulawreview.org/DWhaley.pdf

Made in the USA
Monee, IL
13 September 2026

62975574R00100